THE
CALM
WITHIN

Timeless Techniques for Inner Peace and Resilience

FELIX GRAYSON

MINDSPARK
PUBLISHING

To those who seek stillness amidst the storm—
May you always find the calm within.

"You cannot control the events of the world, but you can control your response to them. That is where your power lies."

— *Marcus Aurelius*

ABOUT STONED PHILOSOPHER

Welcome to the *Stoned Philosopher* series—where timeless wisdom meets the modern world.

Each book distills powerful lessons from history's greatest minds, leaders, and thinkers—transforming their ideas into practical insights for today's challenges.

From mastering habits, calm, and resilience to understanding success, leadership, and meaning, this collection invites you to think deeper, live wiser, and see life from new perspectives.

Whether you're exploring *Modern Zen*, uncovering *The Wisdom of Warriors*, or seeking clarity through *The Art of Perspective*, every title offers a journey toward self-mastery and understanding.

Discover the full *Stoned Philosopher* collection and more at **FelixGrayson.com**, home of **Mind-Spark Publishing**—where knowledge, philosophy, and storytelling come together to spark lifelong curiosity.

FelixGrayson.com

Wisdom isn't something we find—it's something we grow into.

Let the journey begin.

CONTENTS

INTRODUCTION: THE CALM WITHIN

Imagine standing in the eye of a storm. Around you, chaos reigns—winds howl, waves crash, and the sky churns with fury. Yet within this center, there is an unshakable stillness. The storm does not touch it. This is the image of inner peace: not the absence of chaos, but the ability to remain steady and calm in its midst.

Our lives, too, often resemble storms. Deadlines, obligations, conflicts, and uncertainties swirl around us, pulling at our attention and testing our resilience. In this modern age, where the pace of life seems to quicken with every passing day, the idea of calm can feel elusive, even unattainable. But what if I told you that calm is not a distant shore you must strive to reach, but a place you already possess within yourself?

This book is an invitation to rediscover that calm—to explore the practices, perspectives, and principles that allow you to navigate life with greater clarity, resilience, and peace. It is a journey inward, where the tools for harmony have always been waiting.

Why We Seek Peace

From the dawn of human existence, we have sought answers to the chaos of life. Ancient philosophers pondered the nature of happiness, theologians explored the essence of the soul, and artists captured the beauty of stillness in their work. Despite our varied approaches, the questions remain the same: How can we find peace in a world filled with uncertainty? How can we weather life's inevitable storms without losing ourselves?

The need for inner calm is universal. It transcends cultures, time periods, and circumstances. Whether we are managing the demands of a career, nurturing relationships, or navigating personal challenges, we all yearn for a sense of balance—a place where we can feel grounded, even when life feels overwhelming.

The good news is that this place is not a mythical ideal or a privilege reserved for the few. It is accessible to all of us, regardless of our circumstances. The path to peace is not about escaping life's difficulties; it is about transforming the way we experience them.

The Journey Ahead

In these pages, we will explore the timeless practices and perspectives that foster inner calm. Drawing on philosophy, psychology, and personal growth, this book weaves together ancient wisdom and modern insights to offer a practical guide for navigating life's challenges.

Each chapter is a stepping stone on this journey:

- We begin by examining the roots of inner turmoil and how to cultivate awareness of the patterns that disrupt our peace. Understanding the nature of the storm is the first step toward finding the stillness within it.

- Next, we delve into the art of stillness, exploring how moments of reflection and mindfulness can anchor us in the present and restore clarity.

- We then turn to resilience, uncovering the mindset shifts and practices that empower us to grow stronger through adversity.

- Letting go becomes the focus of our exploration, as we learn to release emotional burdens and embrace acceptance as a path to freedom.

- Nature, too, offers its wisdom, teaching us how to reconnect with its rhythms and find solace in its embrace.

- From there, we move to balance—discovering how to harmonize life's demands while staying true to our values and priorities.

- Rituals, those small yet powerful acts of intention, guide us in creating a daily foundation for inner calm.

- Finally, we examine how to sustain peace amidst chaos, finding meaning in our journey and sharing it with others to create a ripple effect of positivity.

These chapters are not a prescription but an invitation to reflect, experiment, and integrate what resonates with you. This is your journey, and the practices you adopt will be as unique as your life.

A Timeless Pursuit

The pursuit of peace is not new. Every era of human history has grappled with its own forms of chaos, and every era has produced thinkers, leaders, and visionaries who found ways to transcend it. Marcus Aurelius wrote his *Meditations* amidst the pressures of ruling an empire. The Buddha taught detachment and mindfulness in a world of suffering. Modern psychologists study resilience and emotional regulation in the context of today's challenges. These voices from across time remind us that while the storms may change, the need for inner calm remains constant.

What has also remained constant is the wisdom that calm begins within. It is not something we can impose on the world or demand from others; it is something we cultivate in ourselves. This cultivation is a lifelong journey, one that deepens with practice and intention.

The Gift of Calm

Inner peace is not just a gift to yourself—it is a gift to the world. When you cultivate calm within, you influence the people around you. Your presence becomes a source of stability, your actions a reflection of compassion. The ripple effect of your peace extends outward, creating connections, fostering understanding, and inspiring others to find their own calm.

This is perhaps the most profound reason to pursue peace: its ability to transform not just your life, but the lives of those you touch. In a world that often feels divided and chaotic, the calm within each of us can be a force for unity and hope.

An Invitation

As you embark on this journey, I invite you to approach it with curiosity and openness. You do not need to have all the answers or achieve perfection. The practices and perspectives in this book are not about creating a life without challenges; they are about equipping you to meet those challenges with strength, clarity, and grace.

Take what resonates, experiment with what feels unfamiliar, and allow the process to unfold naturally. Growth is not linear, and peace is not a destination—it is a way of being. Trust that each step you take, no matter how small, brings you closer to the calm within.

The storm will always be there. But so, too, will the stillness at its center.

Welcome to the journey.

CHAPTER 1: THE STORM INSIDE – UNDERSTANDING INNER TURMOIL

The Roots of Inner Chaos

In the quiet moments of our lives—between the noise of obligations, the hum of technology, and the clamor of the world—chaos often finds fertile ground. It whispers doubts, stirs fears, and magnifies stresses, until what lies within us feels as turbulent as the most violent storm. But chaos, for all its overwhelming force, is not born of nothing. Its roots stretch deep into the soil of human experience, nourished by the pressures of modern life and the timeless struggles of the human mind.

At the heart of inner chaos lies a clash of worlds: the one we inhabit and the one we imagine. Stress, anxiety, and discontent are often the byproducts of this tension. Consider the pace of today's world—its relentless demands and ever-present uncertainties. The pressure to achieve, to belong, to be enough, presses down on us, inflaming a sense of inadequacy. Ancient philosophers like Epicurus recognized this phenomenon in his meditations on contentment, warning against a life consumed by unbridled desires and external validation. "It is not what we have," he wrote, "but what we enjoy, that constitutes our abundance."

In many ways, humanity has not changed. The arenas of competition may differ, but the battles—over status, identity, and control—remain the same. Stress is the body's natural response to perceived threats, a mechanism that once kept our ancestors alive in the face of predators. Yet, in the absence of saber-toothed tigers, these triggers have evolved into far subtler threats: the ping of a missed email, the gaze of a disapproving colleague, or the nagging sense that others are living a better, more fulfilled life.

Anxiety, similarly, is a future-focused fear. It thrives in the gap between where we are and where we think we should be. Marcus Aurelius, the Stoic emperor of Rome, often wrote of this tension in his private journals. "You have power over your mind," he reminded himself. "Realize this, and you will find strength." In these words lies a timeless truth: much of our inner chaos is not the product of external events but the narratives we construct about them.

To unravel this chaos, we must first understand its origins. Often, the seeds of turmoil are sown in childhood, where unspoken expectations and learned behaviors take root. A child who grows up in an environment where success is valued over effort may internalize the belief that failure is a reflection of worth, not growth. Similarly, those who witness conflict or experience instability may carry a heightened sensitivity to rejection or uncertainty into adulthood.

These early experiences shape our triggers — the situations or interactions that provoke intense emotional responses. For some, it might be the fear of criticism; for others, the dread of loneliness. Identifying these triggers is the first step in dismantling their power. Reflecting on one's past with curiosity, rather than judgment, allows us to see how these patterns were formed and why they persist.

But external forces also play a significant role in the cultivation of chaos. The modern world is an unrelenting source of stimulation. Notifications demand our attention. News headlines bombard us with crises. Social media creates an endless reel of comparisons. It is no surprise, then, that the nervous system — designed for brief bursts of alertness — struggles to sustain this constant onslaught. As the psychologist Daniel Kahneman observed, the mind is a limited resource, prone to depletion when overtaxed by decision-making, vigilance, and fear.

This overstimulation leads to what some philosophers and scientists describe as "cognitive overload." The brain, overwhelmed by competing inputs, struggles to prioritize, leaving us scattered and reactive. In such a state, even small inconveniences—a misplaced key, a terse comment from a friend—can trigger outsized emotional reactions.

And yet, for all its apparent inevitability, chaos is not insurmountable. Understanding its roots gives us the tools to confront it. When we acknowledge the role of external pressures, we can begin to question their authority over us. Must we check every notification, respond to every demand, and meet every expectation? When we examine the stories we tell ourselves, we uncover the assumptions and beliefs that keep us trapped in cycles of anxiety and stress.

Perhaps the most profound lesson comes from recognizing that chaos, while disruptive, is also a teacher. Like a storm that clears the air, it forces us to confront what we might otherwise ignore. It reveals where we are vulnerable, what we value, and where we must grow. By facing it with courage and curiosity, we begin the journey toward calm—a journey not of escape, but of transformation.

Inner peace does not come from silencing the storm but from learning to navigate it. It is the result of understanding, not avoidance. The roots of chaos may run deep, but so too does our capacity for resilience and clarity. And in the chapters to come, we will explore the tools and techniques that have helped countless individuals—from ancient sages to modern seekers—find their way through the storm, into the calm within.

The Role of the Mind in Conflict

The human mind is both a sanctuary and a battlefield. It possesses the remarkable ability to create beauty and harmony but also harbors the potential to stir chaos and conflict. When inner turmoil arises, it is often the mind itself that amplifies the storm, turning small waves into crashing tsunamis. Understanding the mind's role in perpetuating this chaos is essential to taming it.

The ancient Stoics were among the first to articulate this idea. Epictetus, a slave turned philosopher, observed, "Men are disturbed not by things, but by the views they take of them." These words, written nearly two millennia ago, resonate deeply today. The Stoics believed that external events, no matter how challenging or painful, hold no power over our emotional state. Instead, it is our interpretation of these events—the meaning we assign to them—that determines their impact.

Imagine two people caught in a sudden rainstorm. One curses their misfortune, feeling angry and inconvenienced. The other laughs, finding joy in the unexpected experience. The rain is the same, but their minds frame it differently. This distinction illustrates the mind's role in creating either conflict or calm. When we perceive life's challenges as personal affronts or insurmountable obstacles, we fuel our inner turmoil. But when we shift our perspective, we open the door to resilience and peace.

Modern cognitive psychology echoes these ancient teachings. Cognitive Behavioral Therapy (CBT), one of the most effective forms of psychotherapy, is built on the premise that our thoughts shape our emotions and behaviors. Aaron Beck, the father of CBT, identified patterns of distorted thinking that often lead to unnecessary stress and conflict. These cognitive distortions—such as catastrophizing, black-and-white thinking, or overgeneralization—are traps that ensnare the mind. For example, a single criticism at work might lead someone to believe they are entirely incompetent, spiraling into self-doubt and anxiety.

These thought patterns, while automatic, are not immutable. With awareness and practice, we can challenge and reframe them. Recognizing that a fleeting thought is just that—a thought, not an objective truth—can create space between our experiences and our reactions. This space is where transformation begins.

The mind's role in conflict is further compounded by its preference for certainty. Uncertainty triggers discomfort, as the brain instinctively

seeks patterns and predictability to feel secure.
However, life is rarely predictable, and this mis-
match creates fertile ground for inner strife. The
Buddhist concept of "monkey mind" aptly describes this phenomenon: the restless, chattering
mind that swings from worry to doubt, unable
to rest.

The solution, according to both ancient wisdom
and modern science, lies in cultivating mindfulness. By anchoring our awareness in the present
moment, we can quiet the monkey mind and
break free from the grip of unhelpful thought
patterns. Mindfulness is not about suppressing
thoughts but observing them with curiosity and
detachment. A thought that might have triggered anger or fear becomes a passing cloud,
acknowledged but not engaged.

Historical figures provide compelling examples
of the power of mastering the mind. Marcus Aurelius, the Stoic emperor, faced immense pressures as the ruler of a vast and often fractious
empire. His personal writings, compiled in *Meditations*, reveal a man constantly grappling with
the role of his mind in shaping his experience.
"You have power over your mind," he wrote.

"Not outside events. Realize this, and you will find strength." These words reflect a deliberate practice of reframing challenges and focusing on what lies within his control.

The practice of reframing is a powerful tool for modern readers as well. When faced with conflict, we can ask: Is this situation as dire as my mind perceives it to be? What alternative interpretations exist? By consciously shifting our perspective, we disrupt the automatic pathways of fear and negativity that the mind often defaults to.

Another critical aspect of the mind's role in conflict is its attachment to identity and ego. Much of our inner turmoil arises from perceived threats to how we see ourselves. A harsh critique, a failed project, or even a minor slight can feel like an attack on our very essence. The ego, desperate to protect its image, reacts defensively, turning small issues into major conflicts.

Here, the teachings of Eastern philosophy offer profound insight. The Bhagavad Gita, a cornerstone of Hindu wisdom, speaks to the importance of detachment from the ego's demands.

"Perform your duty with equanimity," it advises, "without attachment to the fruits of action." By shifting our focus from outcomes to actions, we free ourselves from the mind's relentless need for validation and approval.

Practicing detachment does not mean apathy or indifference. Instead, it involves recognizing that our worth is not tied to external achievements or opinions. When we internalize this truth, the mind loses much of its power to create unnecessary conflict.

Ultimately, the mind's role in inner turmoil is both the problem and the solution. It is the source of distorted perceptions, but it also holds the key to clarity and peace. By understanding how the mind operates—its biases, habits, and vulnerabilities—we can begin to reclaim our inner world.

Inner calm is not about silencing the mind but guiding it. Like a skilled sailor navigating turbulent waters, we can learn to steer our thoughts and emotions with intention. The storm may rage around us, but with practice, the mind can become an anchor, holding us steady in even the most chaotic seas.

Emotional Weather Patterns

Emotions, like weather, are ever-changing—sometimes a gentle breeze, other times a ferocious storm. They are unpredictable and, at times, overwhelming, but they are also natural. This metaphor of emotional weather is not merely poetic; it offers a lens through which we can understand and navigate the complexities of our inner lives. Just as we prepare for and respond to shifts in the weather, we can learn to recognize and manage our emotional climates with greater wisdom and grace.

The analogy of emotions as weather has deep roots in philosophy and psychology. Ancient Greek thinkers like Aristotle viewed emotions as integral to the human experience, neither inherently good nor bad, but powerful forces that must be understood and moderated. More recently, psychologist Paul Ekman identified six basic emotions—happiness, sadness, anger, fear, surprise, and disgust—that, like fundamental weather patterns, shape the landscape of our emotional experience. Understanding

these emotions and their triggers is the first step
toward navigating them effectively.

Consider a stormy day. The clouds gather, the
winds rise, and rain begins to fall. To an unpre-
pared observer, this sudden change might feel
overwhelming or even threatening. Similarly,
emotions can seem to come out of nowhere,
taking us by surprise and leaving us unsure
of how to respond. But just as meteorologists
study weather patterns to predict and prepare
for storms, we can learn to observe and anticipate our emotional states, reducing their power
to destabilize us.

One of the most valuable tools for navigating
emotional weather is self-awareness. Much like
watching the sky for signs of an approaching
storm, paying attention to our internal cues—
tension in the body, racing thoughts, or a sudden shift in mood—can help us identify the
early signs of emotional turbulence. The practice of mindfulness, rooted in Buddhist teachings, trains us to observe these changes without
judgment. By acknowledging emotions as they
arise, we create space between the feeling and
our reaction, allowing us to respond with clarity

rather than impulsivity.

Take anger, for example. Often described as a "hot" emotion, anger can feel like a sudden heatwave, flaring up and consuming our attention. The Stoics, particularly Seneca, warned of the destructive power of unchecked anger, comparing it to a raging fire. However, they also emphasized that anger, like fire, can be controlled and even harnessed. Recognizing the early signs of anger—a tightening of the chest, a quickening pulse—gives us an opportunity to pause, reflect, and choose a measured response rather than reacting in the heat of the moment.

Similarly, sadness can be likened to a heavy fog, obscuring our perspective and making it difficult to see a way forward. In such moments, it is easy to become lost in the gloom, believing it will never lift. Yet, as any weather-worn traveler knows, fog eventually clears. By acknowledging sadness without resistance—allowing ourselves to feel it while also remembering its impermanence—we can navigate it with greater resilience. Practices such as journaling or speaking with a trusted friend can serve as guiding lights, helping us find clarity amidst the haze.

Not all emotional weather is stormy, of course. Joy and contentment, akin to sunny days, bring light and warmth to our lives. Yet, even these emotions must be approached with mindfulness. As the philosopher Heraclitus observed, "Everything flows." Clinging too tightly to happiness can lead to disappointment when it inevitably wanes, just as expecting perpetual sunshine is unrealistic. Embracing the transient nature of all emotions allows us to savor the good moments while remaining grounded when they pass.

One of the most important lessons from the weather metaphor is the concept of acceptance. Just as we cannot control the rain or the wind, we cannot force our emotions to disappear. Resistance—whether it takes the form of denial, suppression, or avoidance—only intensifies the storm. Instead, we must learn to coexist with our emotions, treating them as temporary visitors rather than permanent fixtures. The mindfulness practice of "noting" is particularly useful in this regard: simply naming the emotion ("anger," "sadness," "fear") without attaching a story to it can help us acknowledge its presence without being overwhelmed by it.

Historical figures have often drawn on this wisdom in moments of great emotional challenge. Viktor Frankl, a Holocaust survivor and psychiatrist, wrote extensively about the power of choosing one's attitude in the face of suffering. In his seminal work, *Man's Search for Meaning*, Frankl described how even in the darkest of circumstances, he found moments of inner peace by accepting his emotions and focusing on what lay within his control. His experience illustrates that while we cannot always change the external weather, we can cultivate an inner climate of resilience and purpose.

Practical strategies for navigating emotional weather include grounding techniques, which anchor us in the present moment when emotions threaten to sweep us away. Breathing exercises, such as the 4-7-8 method (inhaling for four counts, holding for seven, and exhaling for eight), can help calm the nervous system and create a sense of stability. Visualization is another powerful tool: imagining emotions as passing clouds or waves lapping at the shore can remind us of their transience, reducing their intensity.

Another approach is to develop a "weather report" for your emotions, much like meteorologists track atmospheric conditions. This involves checking in with yourself regularly throughout the day, noting your emotional state and any contributing factors. Over time, patterns may emerge, helping you anticipate and prepare for emotional storms before they fully develop. For example, you might notice that lack of sleep leads to heightened irritability or that certain environments trigger anxiety. Armed with this knowledge, you can take proactive steps to protect your emotional well-being.

Ultimately, the metaphor of emotional weather teaches us that emotions are not enemies to be vanquished but natural phenomena to be understood and embraced. By observing our inner weather with curiosity and compassion, we can navigate its fluctuations with greater ease and resilience. The storm may still come, but with preparation and practice, we can stand firm in its midst, confident in the knowledge that calm skies will return.

Beginning the Journey to Calm

Every journey begins with a single step, yet the path to inner peace can feel daunting when standing at the edge of turmoil. The prospect of calm might seem distant, obscured by the weight of past experiences, the pull of unhelpful habits, and the demands of modern life. Yet, calm is not a far-off destination; it is a skill to be cultivated, one small, deliberate action at a time. By understanding the nature of inner peace and adopting practices that foster it, we can begin the transformation from chaos to clarity.

The ancient Chinese philosopher Lao Tzu likened life's journey to the flow of water: gentle yet persistent, shaping even the hardest stone over time. His teaching reminds us that inner peace is not achieved in grand, sweeping gestures but through quiet, consistent effort. Calm, like water, flows from the choices we make each day—the way we approach challenges, nurture ourselves, and engage with the world.

To begin this journey, it is essential to redefine what inner peace means. Too often, peace is mistaken for the absence of struggle or the complete elimination of negative emotions. This notion is as misleading as expecting the weather to remain perpetually sunny. True calm does not mean avoiding storms; it means learning to navigate them with steadiness and grace. Peace arises not from controlling the external world but from cultivating a sense of stability within.

One of the first steps on this journey is recognizing that calm is a skill, not an inherent trait. It is tempting to believe that some people are simply born more peaceful, while others are destined to wrestle with constant unrest. Yet, history and psychology tell a different story. Inner peace, like any skill, can be learned, practiced, and strengthened over time. Nelson Mandela, for example, endured 27 years of imprisonment without succumbing to bitterness or despair. His calm resolve was not a product of circumstance but a testament to his inner work—his ability to find purpose, maintain perspective, and focus on what he could control.

As we embark on this journey, self-compassion becomes a vital companion. It is easy to grow impatient or critical when progress feels slow, but such attitudes only add to the weight we carry. The Buddhist teacher Thich Nhat Hanh often spoke of treating oneself as one would a dear friend—with kindness, understanding, and encouragement. "Smile, breathe, and go slowly," he advised, emphasizing that the path to peace is as much about the process as the destination.

The journey to calm also requires an openness to growth. Just as a seed must break through the soil to reach the light, we must confront and transcend our old patterns to cultivate peace. This process often involves unlearning habits of mind that perpetuate chaos, such as dwelling on the past, catastrophizing the future, or seeking validation in external achievements. By becoming aware of these patterns, we can begin to replace them with healthier practices that nurture calm and resilience.

Central to this transformation is the practice of mindfulness—the art of paying attention to the present moment without judgment. Mindfulness anchors us in the here and now, allowing us to observe our thoughts and emotions without being swept away by them. It is the foundation upon which inner peace is built, offering clarity amid confusion and calm amid turmoil. Even a few moments of mindful breathing each day can create space for reflection and reset the mind.

But mindfulness is only the beginning. The tools
and techniques for cultivating calm are as diverse as the challenges we face. For some, journaling provides a space to untangle thoughts and
process emotions. For others, physical movement—whether yoga, tai chi, or a simple walk
in nature—restores a sense of balance. Practices
such as gratitude, visualization, and breathwork offer additional pathways to peace, each
tailored to different temperaments and needs.

Historical and philosophical insights further
illuminate this journey. The Stoics, for example,
emphasized the importance of focusing on what
lies within our control. Marcus Aurelius advised,
"You have power over your mind—not outside
events. Realize this, and you will find strength."
This perspective encourages us to shift our energy away from resisting what we cannot change
and toward cultivating the qualities that sustain
inner peace: patience, courage, and clarity.

Similarly, the Japanese concept of wabi-sabi—
the appreciation of imperfection and impermanence—offers a profound lesson in acceptance.

Life's uncertainties and imperfections are not obstacles to peace but opportunities to practice it. By embracing the beauty of the present moment, however incomplete or messy it may seem, we can find calm in even the most unexpected places.

Community also plays a crucial role in this journey. While inner peace is deeply personal, it is not achieved in isolation. Surrounding ourselves with supportive relationships—whether friends, family, or like-minded individuals—creates an environment where calm can flourish. Conversations that inspire, laughter that lightens the heart, and shared moments of quiet connection all contribute to the cultivation of peace.

Finally, beginning the journey to calm requires a commitment to consistency. Like physical fitness, mental and emotional well-being depend on regular practice. Small, daily actions—a moment of gratitude, a mindful breath, a kind word—build over time, creating a foundation of resilience that can withstand life's storms. These practices may seem insignificant at first, but their cumulative effect is profound.

As we explore the tools and techniques for cultivating calm in the chapters ahead, it is important to remember that the journey itself is part of the transformation. Each step—no matter how small—moves us closer to the calm within. By approaching this journey with patience, curiosity, and determination, we can begin to reshape our inner world, finding strength not in the absence of struggle but in our ability to navigate it with grace.

The path to inner peace is not a straight line. It will have detours and setbacks, moments of doubt and frustration. Yet, with each step, we learn and grow. We discover that calm is not something we find; it is something we create. And in creating it, we not only transform ourselves but also radiate a sense of peace that touches the world around us.

CHAPTER 2: THE STILLNESS FACTOR – THE POWER OF SILENCE AND REFLECTION

The Philosophy of Stillness

In a world defined by speed and noise, stillness feels like a radical act. It stands in quiet defiance of the relentless demands of modern life, offering a space where the mind can rest and the soul can breathe. Yet, stillness is more than mere inactivity; it is a profound state of being, a doorway to clarity, wisdom, and peace. Across cultures and centuries, philosophers, mystics, and spiritual leaders have turned to stillness as a path to self-discovery and enlightenment, recognizing its timeless relevance in the pursuit of inner calm.

The roots of stillness run deep in the human story. In ancient China, Lao Tzu wrote, "Silence is a source of great strength." For Lao Tzu, stillness was not an absence but a presence—an active engagement with the essence of life. He observed that in stillness, the natural order reveals itself, unclouded by the distractions of the mind. This idea became a cornerstone of Taoist philosophy, which teaches that by aligning with the flow of life, rather than resisting it, we discover harmony and balance.

Similarly, in the Christian tradition, stillness is celebrated as a way to commune with the divine. The contemplative practices of early Christian mystics, such as silent prayer and meditation, were not merely acts of devotion but tools for deep reflection and connection. Saint Augustine wrote, "You have made us for yourself, O Lord, and our heart is restless until it rests in you." For Augustine and many others, stillness was a means of transcending the restlessness of the world, grounding oneself in a higher truth.

The Zen tradition of Buddhism also places stillness at its heart. Zen masters teach that silence is not simply the absence of noise but a state of attentive presence. In Zen meditation, or zazen, practitioners sit in quiet awareness, observing their thoughts without attachment. This practice, deceptively simple in its execution, is profoundly transformative. It reveals the mind's habitual patterns and opens a space where true insight can emerge. As Zen master Shunryu Suzuki famously said, "In the beginner's mind there are many possibilities, but in the expert's mind there are few." Stillness, for Zen practitioners, is the beginner's mind—a fertile ground for growth and understanding.

Despite its ancient roots, the philosophy of still-ness remains strikingly relevant today. Modern life, with its constant stimulation and demands, often leaves little room for quiet reflection. The pace of technology, the pressure to perform, and the endless stream of information create a kind of mental clutter that can cloud judgment and exhaust the spirit. Yet, as the ancients under-stood, stillness is not a luxury but a necessity. It is a counterbalance to the chaos, a sanctuary where we can find ourselves again.

One of the most profound aspects of stillness is its universality. It transcends culture, religion, and philosophy, resonating with anyone who seeks peace and clarity. The practice of stillness can take many forms, from the disciplined med-itation of a Zen monk to the quiet contemplation of a poet walking in nature. What unites these practices is their shared goal: to quiet the mind and open the heart.

The transformative power of stillness lies in its ability to reconnect us with the present moment. When we are still, we become aware of the sub-tle rhythms of life—the beating of our heart, the rustle of leaves in the wind, the warmth of the sun on our skin. These experiences, often overlooked in the rush of daily life, ground us in the here and now. They remind us that life is not something to be chased or achieved but something to be lived and experienced fully.

Historical figures offer powerful examples of how stillness can shape a life. Mahatma Gandhi, for instance, was known for his practice of silence. Every Monday, he observed a day of silence, using the time to reflect and recharge. Gandhi believed that stillness was essential for clarity and strength, enabling him to lead with conviction and purpose. His commitment to silence was not an escape from the world but a way of engaging with it more deeply.

Another example is the American transcendentalist Henry David Thoreau, who famously retreated to Walden Pond to live simply and observe life's essence. In his seminal work, *Walden*, Thoreau wrote, "I never found the companion that was so companionable as solitude." His time in stillness allowed him to strip away the superficial and connect with the profound, offering insights that continue to inspire generations.

For those new to the practice of stillness, the idea of sitting in silence can feel daunting. The mind, accustomed to constant stimulation, often resists the quiet, filling the space with chatter and distraction. But this discomfort is part of the process. Like a jar of muddy water, the mind needs time to settle. As the sediment falls away, clarity emerges, revealing the still waters beneath.

Stillness does not require a monastery or a mountaintop. It can be found in the small moments of everyday life—a quiet morning with a cup of tea, a few deep breaths before a meeting, or a walk without a destination. These moments, though brief, have the power to transform our relationship with ourselves and the world around us.

In the chapters ahead, we will explore how stillness can be cultivated and integrated into daily life. From ancient practices like Zen meditation and Christian contemplative prayer to modern techniques supported by science, the tools for achieving stillness are as varied as they are effective. By embracing the philosophy of stillness, we begin a journey not only toward calm but toward a deeper understanding of who we are and what it means to live with intention.

Stillness is not the absence of movement but the presence of awareness. It is a state of being that allows us to pause, reflect, and reconnect with what truly matters. In the stillness, we discover the strength to weather life's storms and the wisdom to navigate its complexities. And in doing so, we find a peace that transcends the noise—a calm that endures.

The Science Behind Silence

Silence is often perceived as a void, an absence of sound and activity. Yet, modern science reveals that silence is far from empty; it is a powerful force with profound effects on the brain and body. The act of quieting the mind, whether through mindfulness, meditation, or simple moments of stillness, initiates a cascade of neurological and physiological benefits. These findings affirm what ancient traditions have long understood: silence is not merely restorative; it is transformative.

The human brain is constantly active, processing sensory input, forming thoughts, and reacting to the world. This ceaseless activity, while vital for survival, comes at a cost. Studies in neuroscience have shown that excessive mental stimulation leads to heightened stress levels, impaired focus, and reduced emotional regulation. Silence, however, offers a remedy. By stepping away from the noise, both external and internal, we allow the brain to reset and recalibrate.

One of the most compelling discoveries about silence comes from research on the brain's default mode network (DMN). The DMN is a network of interconnected brain regions that becomes active when we are at rest and not focused on external tasks. It is during these moments of quiet that the brain engages in self-reflection, memory consolidation, and creative problem-solving. Neuroscientist Marcus Raichle, who first identified the DMN, described it as the brain's "silent engine," essential for understanding ourselves and navigating our lives. Moments of stillness, then, are not unproductive pauses but crucial opportunities for mental rejuvenation.

Beyond its role in reflection, silence has measurable benefits for stress reduction. Chronic stress, often exacerbated by constant noise and mental clutter, activates the body's fight-or-flight response, flooding the system with stress hormones like cortisol. Over time, this state of hyperarousal can lead to health problems, including anxiety, depression, and cardiovascular disease. Silence, by contrast, activates the parasympathetic nervous system, the body's "rest and digest" mode. This shift calms the heart rate, lowers blood pressure, and reduces cortisol levels, creating a physiological state conducive to healing and recovery.

One groundbreaking study conducted by Dr. Luciano Bernardi in 2006 examined the effects of different types of sound on the brain. The researchers were surprised to find that two minutes of silence between soundtracks produced greater relaxation and heightened brain activity than even soothing music. This finding suggests that silence is not merely the absence of noise but an active and dynamic state that promotes profound physiological benefits.

The neurological effects of silence extend to cognitive function. A 2013 study by neuroscientists at Duke University found that exposure to two hours of silence daily led to the generation of new cells in the hippocampus, a region of the brain associated with memory and learning. This discovery highlights the potential of silence to enhance neuroplasticity, the brain's ability to adapt and grow throughout life. In a world where information overload often hampers our ability to think clearly and retain knowledge, silence emerges as a tool for sharpening focus and fostering intellectual growth.

These scientific insights resonate deeply with the teachings of mindfulness and meditation, practices that have been refined over millennia. Mindfulness, defined as the practice of bringing one's attention to the present moment, often begins with an embrace of silence. By sitting quietly and observing the breath, practitioners create a space where the mind can settle and gain clarity. Studies on mindfulness meditation consistently show its effectiveness in reducing symptoms of anxiety, depression, and chronic pain. This is partly because meditation trains the brain to regulate its responses to stress, creating a buffer against the pressures of modern life.

One particularly fascinating area of research involves the impact of silence on creativity. The composer Ludwig van Beethoven was known to retreat into nature for hours of solitude, allowing the quiet to inspire his symphonies. Modern psychologists have found that silence facilitates divergent thinking, a cognitive process associated with generating creative ideas. By reducing external distractions, silence allows the brain to explore new connections and possibilities, fostering innovation and insight.

The benefits of silence are not limited to extended periods of quiet. Even brief moments of stillness can have a profound impact. Dr. Herbert Benson, a pioneer in mind-body medicine, developed the concept of the relaxation response, a physiological state triggered by practices like deep breathing and meditation. Benson's research demonstrated that as little as ten minutes of focused silence each day could significantly reduce stress and improve overall well-being. This finding underscores the accessibility of silence as a tool for transformation; it does not require hours of solitude but can be woven into the fabric of daily life.

Despite these compelling benefits, silence can feel elusive in a world dominated by noise. The constant hum of technology, the demands of work, and the chatter of social media create an environment where quiet is often drowned out. Yet, the very act of seeking silence is itself a step toward reclaiming balance. By consciously carving out moments of stillness—turning off notifications, stepping outside, or simply pausing to breathe—we create a sanctuary for the mind.

The science of silence also invites us to rethink our relationship with sound. Noise pollution, defined as unwanted or harmful sound, has been shown to have detrimental effects on health, from increased stress to impaired cognitive performance. Silence, in contrast, offers a counterbalance, reminding us that sound and stillness are not opposites but partners. Just as a piece of music is shaped by the pauses between the notes, our lives gain meaning and depth from the moments of quiet that punctuate our days.

Ultimately, the science behind silence affirms what ancient traditions have long known: stillness is not a void but a source of strength. It is a state that nourishes the brain, calms the body, and opens the heart. By embracing silence, we do more than reduce noise; we create space for growth, healing, and connection. In the chapters to come, we will explore practical ways to integrate the power of silence into daily life, drawing on both ancient wisdom and modern science to guide the journey.

Techniques for Practicing Stillness

Stillness is a paradoxical skill. At first, it may seem elusive, especially in a world filled with constant distractions and demands. Yet, it is within reach for anyone willing to cultivate it. The art of stillness does not require grand gestures or perfect circumstances; it begins with small, intentional practices that anchor the mind and calm the spirit. By weaving these techniques into daily life, we can create moments of peace that ripple outward, transforming our experience of the world.

One of the simplest and most effective ways to practice stillness is through breathwork. Breathing, while automatic, is also a powerful tool for self-regulation. Ancient traditions recognized this long before modern science confirmed it. In yoga, the practice of pranayama—controlled breathing—is used to balance energy and focus the mind. Similarly, Zen meditation emphasizes the breath as a gateway to presence. A common technique involves observing each inhale and exhale, allowing the rhythm of the breath to ground the mind in the present moment. This practice, though straightforward, has profound effects. Research shows that slow, intentional breathing activates the parasympathetic nervous system, reducing stress and promoting a sense of calm.

A specific breathwork exercise known as the 4-7-8 method offers a practical entry point. Developed by Dr. Andrew Weil, this technique involves inhaling for four counts, holding the breath for seven counts, and exhaling slowly for eight counts. The extended exhale, in particular, signals the body to relax, making this method ideal for moments of tension or overwhelm. Regular practice of the 4-7-8 method not only calms the mind but also trains the nervous system to respond more effectively to stress over time.

Micro-meditations are another accessible way to incorporate stillness into even the busiest schedule. Unlike traditional meditation, which may require extended periods of quiet, micro-meditations can be practiced in as little as one or two minutes. These brief pauses are an opportunity to reset and refocus, whether at the start of the day, during a work break, or before bed. A simple micro-meditation might involve closing the eyes, taking a few deep breaths, and bringing attention to a single point of focus, such as the sensation of the breath or the sound of nearby birdsong. Over time, these small moments of stillness accumulate, creating a foundation of calm that supports resilience and clarity.

Visualization is another powerful technique for cultivating stillness. The mind, when guided, has the remarkable ability to create a sense of peace, even in the midst of external chaos. Visualization practices often involve imagining a calming scene—a serene forest, a quiet beach, or a starlit sky—and allowing oneself to become immersed in its details. The sound of rustling leaves, the scent of salt in the air, or the feel of cool grass beneath bare feet can transport the mind to a place of tranquility. Neuroscience shows that such imagery activates the same regions of the brain as actual sensory experiences, making visualization an effective tool for reducing stress and enhancing mental clarity.

Nature itself offers a profound stillness that can be both grounding and restorative. The Japanese practice of shinrin-yoku, or "forest bathing," involves immersing oneself in a natural setting and engaging the senses fully. Walking slowly through a forest, noticing the patterns of sunlight on the leaves or the sound of a stream, brings the mind into the present moment and fosters a deep sense of connection. Even if a forest is not nearby, similar benefits can be found in a park, a garden, or simply sitting under a tree. The act of being present in nature is a reminder that stillness is not separate from life but an integral part of it.

Journaling is another practice that can help cultivate stillness, though it operates in a different way. While other techniques focus on quieting the mind, journaling allows thoughts and emotions to flow onto the page, clearing mental clutter and making space for clarity. By setting aside a few minutes each day to write—whether about challenges, gratitude, or reflections—a sense of order begins to emerge. The act of putting pen to paper slows the mind, offering a pause from the relentless stream of thoughts and creating an opportunity to engage with them more intentionally.

The effectiveness of these techniques lies not only in their practice but also in the mindset with which they are approached. The goal is not to achieve perfection but to embrace the process. As Thich Nhat Hanh often taught, even a single mindful breath is a victory. This perspective encourages persistence and patience, recognizing that stillness, like any skill, develops over time.

Historical figures provide inspiring examples of how these practices have been used to cultivate stillness in the face of great challenges. The Roman emperor Marcus Aurelius, for instance, maintained a practice of morning reflection, writing in his journal as a way to ground himself before addressing the demands of his empire. His writings, later compiled as *Meditations*, reveal a man deeply committed to the pursuit of inner peace despite external turmoil. Similarly,

Maya Angelou, the celebrated poet and activist, often spoke of the importance of solitude and self-reflection in her creative process, using quiet moments to channel her thoughts and emotions into powerful expressions of truth.

Modern life presents unique obstacles to stillness, but it also offers unique opportunities. Technology, often criticized for its role in over-stimulation, can also be a tool for cultivating calm. Apps that guide meditation, breathing exercises, or nature sounds can provide structure and support for those new to these practices. However, the key is to use technology intentionally, ensuring it serves as a gateway to stillness rather than a source of distraction.

Ultimately, the techniques for practicing stillness are as varied as the individuals who use them. Whether through breathwork, visualization, journaling, or time spent in nature, the path to stillness is personal and adaptable. What matters most is the commitment to begin—to carve out even a few moments each day to pause, breathe, and reconnect with the present. These small acts, repeated consistently, create a ripple effect that extends far beyond the moment, fostering a sense of peace that carries into all aspects of life.

Stillness is not something we must seek; it is already within us, waiting to be rediscovered. By embracing these techniques, we open ourselves to the possibility of a life lived with greater clarity, resilience, and joy—a life grounded in the calm at our core.

Reflection as a Tool for Clarity

In the rush of daily life, clarity often feels like a distant dream, obscured by a haze of responsibilities, emotions, and noise. Yet clarity is not something we must chase; it is something we cultivate. Reflection, the quiet act of looking inward, offers a way to untangle thoughts and emotions, revealing the deeper truths that lie beneath. Like a still lake that mirrors the sky, reflection allows us to see ourselves and our circumstances more clearly, fostering understanding, growth, and peace.

The power of reflection lies in its ability to create space—space to pause, question, and listen. When we reflect, we step out of the reactive flow of life and into a place of observation. This act, though simple, is transformative. It helps us recognize patterns, understand motivations, and make sense of experiences that might otherwise feel overwhelming. In essence, reflection is the bridge between experience and wisdom, turning the raw material of life into insight.

Historically, reflection has been a cornerstone of many philosophical and spiritual traditions. The ancient Stoics, for example, practiced daily self-examination as a means of aligning their actions with their values. Marcus Aurelius, in his personal writings, often asked himself questions like, "What did I do well today? What could I have done better?" This habit of reflection allowed him to navigate the immense pressures of his role as emperor with a sense of purpose and composure. His reflections, compiled in *Meditations*, continue to inspire readers to this day.

Similarly, in Eastern traditions, reflection is often intertwined with mindfulness and meditation. The Zen practice of "turning the light inward" invites practitioners to observe their thoughts and emotions without judgment, cultivating a sense of curiosity and openness. This reflective process helps dissolve illusions and reveals the underlying nature of the self. As Zen master Thich Nhat Hanh taught, "Understanding is the essence of love. If you cannot understand, you cannot love." Reflection, then, is not just an intellectual exercise but a profound act of self-compassion and connection.

Modern psychology affirms the value of reflection as a tool for emotional regulation and mental clarity. Journaling, in particular, has emerged as a powerful practice for organizing thoughts and processing emotions. Studies show that writing about one's experiences and feelings can reduce stress, improve mood, and enhance problem-solving skills. By externalizing thoughts onto paper, journaling creates a sense of distance, making it easier to analyze and address challenges.

One of the most effective journaling techniques is stream-of-consciousness writing. This involves setting a timer for five or ten minutes and writing continuously, without censoring or editing. The goal is not to produce polished prose but to allow thoughts to flow freely, capturing the raw essence of one's inner world.

This practice often uncovers insights that might otherwise remain hidden, offering a fresh perspective on lingering questions or concerns.

For those seeking a more structured approach, guided journaling prompts can provide direction and focus. Questions like "What am I grateful for today?" or "What lesson can I take from this experience?" encourage reflection on specific aspects of life, fostering a mindset of growth and gratitude. Over time, these small acts of introspection create a cumulative effect, deepening self-awareness and resilience.

Reflection is not limited to the written word. Verbal reflection, whether through conversations with trusted friends or internal dialogue, can also be profoundly clarifying. In the Greek tradition, the philosopher Socrates used questioning as a method of reflection, encouraging his students to examine their beliefs and assumptions. Known as the Socratic Method, this approach emphasizes the importance of inquiry in the pursuit of wisdom. By asking ourselves thoughtful questions — "Why do I feel this way?" "What do I truly want?" — we can uncover deeper layers of understanding and align our actions with our values.

Yet reflection is not always easy. It requires us to confront uncomfortable truths and sit with uncertainty. The temptation to avoid or suppress difficult thoughts can be strong, but avoidance only perpetuates confusion. Reflection, on the other hand, brings clarity by shining a light on the shadows of the mind. As Carl Jung observed, "One does not become enlightened by imagining figures of light, but by making the darkness conscious." Through reflection, we integrate both the light and the dark, creating a more complete and authentic understanding of ourselves.

Nature provides a powerful setting for reflection, offering a sense of stillness and perspective that is difficult to find elsewhere. Walking alone in a quiet park, sitting by a river, or gazing at the stars invites a kind of contemplative state, where thoughts can surface naturally and without pressure. Henry David Thoreau, in his retreat to Walden Pond, found that solitude in nature fostered a deeper connection to his thoughts and values. His reflections, captured in *Walden*, continue to resonate with those seeking simplicity and clarity in a complex world.

Reflection also teaches us to embrace the cyclical nature of life. Just as the moon waxes and wanes, so too do our thoughts and emotions. By observing these cycles, we come to understand that clarity is not a fixed state but a process—one that requires patience and practice. Reflecting on moments of struggle, for example, often reveals their hidden gifts, transforming pain into wisdom and failure into growth. This alchemy of experience is at the heart of reflection's power.

Incorporating reflection into daily life does not require hours of solitude or elaborate rituals. It can be as simple as taking a few moments at the end of each day to ask, "What did I learn today?" or "How did I show up for myself and others?" These small acts of introspection, repeated consistently, create a foundation of clarity that strengthens over time. Reflection, like stillness, is a skill that deepens with practice, offering ever-greater rewards as we continue the journey.

Ultimately, reflection is not about finding definitive answers but about asking meaningful questions. It is a conversation with ourselves, a way of listening to the whispers of the heart and the wisdom of the soul. By embracing reflection as a tool for clarity, we not only navigate life's complexities with greater ease but also connect more deeply with the essence of who we are. And in that connection, we find the clarity we seek—a clarity that guides us toward a life of purpose, peace, and fulfillment.

CHAPTER 3: ANCHORS IN CHAOS – BUILDING RESILIENT MINDSETS

Defining Resilience

Resilience is the quiet strength that allows us to face life's storms without being swept away. It is not the absence of struggle, but the ability to endure, adapt, and grow in the face of adversity. Like an anchor holding a ship steady in turbulent waters, resilience provides the stability we need to navigate challenges and maintain a sense of inner peace. While resilience might seem like a lofty ideal, it is a quality rooted in everyday choices—a mindset and practice that anyone can cultivate.

At its core, resilience is the capacity to recover from difficulties and persist despite setbacks. It is what enables people to rebound from failures, cope with losses, and rise stronger from hardships. Importantly, resilience is not a fixed trait. While some individuals may appear naturally resilient, research shows that resilience is a dynamic skill, one that can be developed through intentional effort and reflection.

Philosophy has long grappled with the nature of resilience. The Stoics, for instance, viewed resilience as an essential component of a good life. They believed that while we cannot control external events, we can control our responses to them. This perspective is encapsulated in the words of Epictetus: "It's not what happens to you, but how you react to it that matters." For the Stoics, resilience was about aligning one's will with the natural flow of life, accepting what cannot be changed, and focusing on what lies within one's power.

One of the most profound historical examples of resilience is found in the life of Viktor Frankl, a psychiatrist and Holocaust survivor. In his memoir, *Man's Search for Meaning*, Frankl recounts how he endured the horrors of concentration camps by finding meaning in his suffering. He observed that those who maintained a sense of purpose—whether through love, faith, or a commitment to something greater than themselves—were more likely to survive and maintain their humanity. Frankl's experience highlights a key aspect of resilience: the ability to find meaning and hope even in the darkest of circumstances.

Modern psychology echoes these insights. Resilience is often described as a combination of traits, such as emotional regulation, optimism, and problem-solving skills, that enable individuals to cope effectively with stress. Dr. Ann Masten, a leading resilience researcher, refers to it as "ordinary magic," emphasizing that resilience is not the result of extraordinary abilities but the interplay of everyday factors like supportive relationships, self-awareness, and adaptability.

One of the most compelling aspects of resilience is its role in achieving inner peace. Life is inherently unpredictable, and no one is immune to setbacks or difficulties. However, resilience transforms these challenges into opportunities for growth and self-discovery. By fostering resilience, we cultivate a sense of trust in our ability to weather life's uncertainties, which in turn reduces anxiety and fosters a deeper sense of calm.

To understand resilience more fully, it is helpful to consider its three core dimensions: recovery, adaptation, and growth. Recovery is the ability to bounce back after a setback, whether it's a personal failure, a health crisis, or a professional disappointment. Adaptation involves adjusting to new circumstances, finding creative solutions to challenges, and maintaining flexibility in the face of change. Growth, perhaps the most transformative dimension, is the process of using adversity as a catalyst for personal development, gaining new insights and strengths as a result.

Consider the analogy of a tree in a storm. A rigid tree, unable to bend with the wind, may snap under the pressure. In contrast, a resilient tree sways with the gusts, its roots anchoring it firmly in the ground. Over time, the stress of the wind strengthens its trunk, making it more robust. Similarly, resilience allows us to remain grounded while adapting to life's challenges, emerging stronger and more capable as a result.

Cultivating resilience begins with self-awareness. By understanding our strengths and vulnerabilities, we can identify the habits, beliefs, and thought patterns that support or undermine our ability to cope with adversity. For instance, a tendency to dwell on past mistakes or catastrophize future outcomes can sap our energy and erode our sense of control. By recognizing these tendencies, we can begin to replace them with more constructive practices, such as focusing on the present moment or reframing challenges as opportunities for growth.

Another essential aspect of resilience is connection. As social beings, we draw strength from our relationships with others. Supportive friendships, family bonds, and community ties provide a safety net that helps us navigate difficult times. In her research on resilience, psychologist Dr. Edith Grotberg found that individuals who actively sought help and maintained close connections were more likely to recover from adversity and maintain their well-being. Connection reminds us that we are not alone in our struggles, offering both comfort and perspective.

Resilience also requires a willingness to embrace discomfort. Growth often occurs at the edge of our comfort zones, where we confront fears, uncertainties, and limitations. This idea is reflected in the Japanese concept of kintsugi, the art of repairing broken pottery with gold. Rather than hiding the cracks, kintsugi celebrates them, transforming the object into something even more beautiful. Similarly, resilience invites us to embrace our imperfections and see our struggles as integral to our journey, not as barriers to our success.

Ultimately, resilience is not about avoiding challenges but engaging with them in a way that
fosters growth and understanding. It is the recognition that while we cannot control the wind,
we can learn to adjust our sails. By cultivating
resilience, we equip ourselves with the tools to
navigate life's uncertainties with courage and
grace, transforming even the harshest storms
into opportunities to anchor ourselves more
deeply in inner peace.

The Mindset Shift

Resilience begins in the mind. While external
circumstances often feel beyond our control, the
way we perceive and respond to them is within
our power to change. This understanding forms
the foundation of the mindset shift—a deliberate reorientation of thought that transforms
challenges into opportunities and failures into
lessons. By reframing difficulties and embracing a growth mindset, we can cultivate mental
toughness and navigate life's complexities with
strength and clarity.

The concept of the growth mindset was popularized by psychologist Dr. Carol Dweck, who identified two distinct ways of thinking: the fixed mindset and the growth mindset. Those with a fixed mindset believe that abilities, intelligence, and potential are static, predetermined qualities. As a result, they often shy away from challenges, viewing failure as a reflection of their limitations. In contrast, those with a growth mindset see challenges as opportunities to learn and develop. They understand that effort, persistence, and adaptability are key to success, and they view setbacks as stepping stones rather than roadblocks.

This shift in perspective is more than an intellectual exercise; it is a profound change in how we approach life. The Roman Stoics were early advocates of this idea, emphasizing the importance of interpreting events through a lens of opportunity rather than defeat. Marcus Aurelius, in his meditations, often reminded himself: "The impediment to action advances action. What stands in the way becomes the way." In other words, obstacles are not barriers to progress but the very means by which we grow stronger.

Consider the story of Thomas Edison, who faced countless failures in his quest to invent the electric light bulb. When asked how he endured repeated setbacks, Edison famously replied, "I have not failed. I've just found 10,000 ways that won't work." His response exemplifies the growth mindset—an unwavering belief in the value of perseverance and the lessons inherent in failure. Edison's mindset not only fueled his innovations but also set a precedent for approaching challenges with curiosity and resilience.

Reframing challenges is central to the mindset shift. This process involves consciously altering the narrative we create about our experiences. For example, a failed project might initially be perceived as a personal shortcoming, evoking feelings of inadequacy or defeat. However, by reframing the situation, we can view it as an opportunity to learn new skills, strengthen problem-solving abilities, or gain insights into areas for improvement. This shift in perspective not only reduces the emotional weight of the setback but also empowers us to move forward with renewed purpose.

The mindset shift also requires a willingness to embrace discomfort. Growth often occurs at the edges of our comfort zones, where we are challenged to stretch beyond what feels safe or familiar. The Japanese concept of *kaizen*, or continuous improvement, reflects this principle. Rather than striving for immediate perfection, *kaizen* emphasizes small, incremental changes that lead to significant progress over time. This approach encourages us to view challenges as manageable steps in a larger journey, fostering a sense of agency and momentum.

Practical strategies for adopting a growth mindset include cultivating self-awareness, practicing gratitude, and setting intentional goals. Self-awareness allows us to recognize when fixed-mindset thinking arises—such as the fear of failure or the tendency to compare ourselves to others—and to counter it with constructive alternatives. Gratitude shifts our focus from what is lacking to what is possible, reminding us of the resources and opportunities already at our disposal. Setting goals provides direction and purpose, transforming abstract aspirations into actionable steps.

Another key aspect of the mindset shift is the role of language. The words we use to describe our experiences shape our perceptions and, ultimately, our reality. For instance, replacing "I can't do this" with "I can't do this yet" introduces a sense of possibility and growth. Similarly, reframing "I failed" as "I learned" reinforces the idea that setbacks are an integral part of progress. These small linguistic changes have a cumulative effect, rewiring the brain to approach challenges with optimism and resilience.

Mindfulness also plays a crucial role in fostering a growth mindset. By cultivating present-moment awareness, we can observe our thoughts without judgment, creating space to choose more constructive responses. Mindfulness teaches us to detach from the automatic narratives of fear or self-doubt, allowing us to approach challenges with clarity and intention. This practice, when combined with deliberate reflection, helps us identify patterns of thought that hinder resilience and replace them with habits that support growth.

Historical figures provide inspiring examples

of the mindset shift in action. Nelson Mandela, during his 27 years of imprisonment, refused to let bitterness or despair define his perspective. Instead, he used his time to reflect, learn, and prepare for the future. Mandela's growth mindset not only sustained him through immense hardship but also enabled him to emerge as a transformative leader, advocating for reconciliation and unity. His life demonstrates the profound power of reframing adversity as an opportunity for growth and impact.

Similarly, Helen Keller, who lost her sight and hearing as a young child, exemplified the strength of a growth mindset. Despite seemingly insurmountable challenges, Keller approached life with curiosity, determination, and gratitude. She once wrote, "Although the world is full of suffering, it is also full of the overcoming of it." Her resilience and optimism continue to inspire countless individuals to embrace their own potential, regardless of the obstacles they face.

The mindset shift does not erase challenges or make them easier, but it transforms the way we relate to them. It teaches us that setbacks are not endpoints but invitations to grow, adapt, and persevere. By adopting a growth mindset, we cultivate the mental toughness needed to face life's uncertainties with courage and grace, building a foundation of resilience that supports both inner peace and lasting fulfillment.

The Power of Perspective

Perspective is a lens through which we view the world, shaping how we interpret events, understand ourselves, and interact with others. It is both deeply personal and profoundly influential, capable of transforming the way we experience life's challenges. By shifting our perspective, we can reduce stress, foster resilience, and navigate adversity with greater clarity and grace.

The power of perspective lies in its ability to reframe our experiences. While we cannot always control the circumstances we face, we can choose how we perceive and respond to them. This idea is central to many philosophical traditions, including Stoicism, which teaches that events are neutral; it is our judgment of them that determines their impact. As Epictetus observed, "It is not what happens to you, but how you react to it that matters." By changing our perspective, we can find opportunity in difficulty and meaning in struggle.

Consider the story of Viktor Frankl, whose perspective transformed his experience of unimaginable suffering. As a prisoner in Nazi concentration camps, Frankl endured extreme deprivation and loss. Yet, rather than succumbing to despair, he chose to focus on the one thing that could not be taken from him: his ability to choose his response. In his seminal work, *Man's Search for Meaning*, Frankl writes, "When we are no longer able to change a situation, we are challenged to change ourselves." By finding purpose in his suffering—whether through imagining future reunions with loved ones or helping fellow prisoners—Frankl demonstrated the profound resilience that a shift in perspective can create.

Modern psychology echoes these insights, emphasizing the importance of cognitive reframing in reducing stress and improving emotional well-being. Cognitive reframing involves consciously challenging negative or unhelpful thoughts and replacing them with more constructive interpretations. For example, a missed opportunity might initially feel like a failure, but reframing it as a chance to learn and grow can transform the experience into a stepping stone for future success. This shift in perspective not only reduces the emotional burden of setbacks but also fosters a sense of agency and optimism.

The power of perspective is also evident in how we interpret challenges. Adversity, though often painful, can serve as a catalyst for growth and transformation. This idea is reflected in the Japanese proverb, "Fall seven times, stand up eight." It reminds us that resilience is not about avoiding difficulties but about rising stronger each time we fall. By viewing challenges as opportunities to develop new skills, deepen self-awareness, or build character, we can approach them with curiosity and determination rather than fear or resistance.

Perspective is not fixed; it is shaped by our beliefs, experiences, and environment. This malleability is both a challenge and an opportunity. On one hand, negative perspectives—such as seeing oneself as a victim or viewing the world as inherently hostile—can perpetuate stress and limit growth. On the other hand, cultivating positive perspectives—such as focusing on gratitude, seeking silver linings, or adopting a long-term view—can enhance resilience and well-being.

Historical figures provide powerful examples of how perspective can transform adversity into triumph. Helen Keller, who lost her sight and hearing at a young age, once described her disabilities as both a challenge and a gift. "Although the world is full of suffering," she wrote, "it is also full of the overcoming of it." Keller's perspective allowed her to approach life with a sense of purpose and possibility, becoming an advocate for social change and a symbol of resilience.

Similarly, Nelson Mandela's perspective during his 27 years of imprisonment was shaped not by bitterness but by hope and determination. Mandela viewed his time in prison as an opportunity to reflect, learn, and prepare for leadership. By focusing on the broader goal of unity and reconciliation, he emerged not as a broken man but as a beacon of resilience and wisdom. Mandela's ability to reframe his experience demonstrates the transformative power of perspective in navigating even the harshest challenges.

Practical strategies for shifting perspective include mindfulness, gratitude, and intentional reflection. Mindfulness helps us observe our thoughts and emotions without judgment, creating space to question unhelpful narratives and adopt more constructive ones. Gratitude shifts our focus from what is lacking to what is present, fostering a sense of abundance and appreciation even in difficult times. Reflecting on past challenges and the growth they inspired can also remind us of our capacity to endure and thrive.

Perspective is particularly powerful in moments of uncertainty or change. When faced with the unknown, it is easy to default to fear or resistance. However, by viewing change as an opportunity for growth rather than a threat, we can approach it with openness and curiosity. This shift in perspective not only reduces stress but also unlocks new possibilities, allowing us to adapt and evolve.

The power of perspective extends beyond individual challenges to encompass our broader worldview. Seeing setbacks as temporary rather than permanent, failures as learning experiences rather than endpoints, and difficulties as opportunities rather than obstacles creates a foundation of resilience. This mindset allows us to move through life with greater confidence and purpose, navigating chaos without losing sight of what truly matters.

Ultimately, perspective is a choice—a decision to see the world not as it appears at first glance but as it can be when viewed through the lens of possibility and growth. By cultivating this choice, we unlock a powerful tool for navigating adversity and building a life of resilience and inner peace. Perspective does not erase challenges, but it transforms our relationship with them, revealing the hidden strengths and opportunities within.

Practices for Strengthening Resilience

Resilience is not a static trait but a dynamic skill, one that grows stronger with practice. Like building physical strength, cultivating resilience requires consistent effort, intentional habits, and a willingness to embrace challenges as opportunities for growth. By incorporating specific practices into daily life, we can strengthen our mental and emotional fortitude, creating a foundation of inner peace that sustains us through life's inevitable storms.

One of the most effective practices for building resilience is cultivating gratitude. Gratitude shifts our focus from what is lacking to what is present, fostering a sense of abundance and appreciation even in difficult times. This practice is rooted in both ancient wisdom and modern science. The Roman philosopher Seneca, for example, wrote extensively about the importance of gratitude, viewing it as a key to contentment and resilience. More recently, psychological studies have shown that practicing gratitude enhances well-being, reduces stress, and improves relationships. Keeping a gratitude journal—writing down three things you are grateful for each day—is a simple yet powerful way to embed this practice into your routine. Over time, it trains the mind to seek and savor the positive, even in the midst of adversity.

Affirmations are another valuable tool for strengthening resilience. These are positive statements that reinforce empowering beliefs about ourselves and our capacity to overcome challenges. While affirmations may seem simplistic, their impact is profound when practiced consistently. Neuroscience reveals that repeated positive affirmations can rewire the brain, replacing self-doubt with confidence and fostering a mindset of possibility. For example, affirmations like "I am capable of handling whatever comes my way" or "I grow stronger through every challenge" can serve as anchors of stability in turbulent times. Writing or speaking these affirmations each morning sets a tone of resilience for the day ahead.

Resilience also thrives on routines that promote self-care and balance. Engaging in regular physical activity, maintaining a healthy diet, and prioritizing sleep are foundational practices that enhance both physical and mental resilience. Exercise, in particular, has been shown to reduce stress, improve mood, and boost cognitive function. Whether it's a brisk walk, a yoga session, or a dance class, movement helps release tension and restore equilibrium. Sleep, too, is a cornerstone of resilience. A well-rested mind is better equipped to navigate stress, make decisions, and regulate emotions. Creating a consistent sleep schedule and establishing bedtime rituals, such as reading or meditating, supports this vital aspect of well-being.

Mindfulness is another cornerstone of resilience, offering a way to ground ourselves in the present moment and navigate challenges with clarity. By practicing mindfulness, we learn to observe our thoughts and emotions without judgment, creating space to respond rather than react. One simple mindfulness exercise involves focusing on the breath, noticing the sensation of each inhale and exhale. This practice anchors the mind in the present, reducing the overwhelm of ruminating on the past or worrying about the future. Over time, mindfulness strengthens our ability to remain calm and centered, even in the face of adversity.

Another effective practice for resilience is reflecting on past challenges and the strengths they revealed. This exercise, known as "strength spotting," involves identifying the qualities—such as perseverance, creativity, or courage—that helped us overcome difficulties in the past. By recognizing these strengths, we build confidence in our ability to face future challenges. Reflecting on these moments also shifts our perspective, reminding us that adversity often brings growth and transformation.

Storytelling, too, plays a vital role in building resilience. The narratives we create about our lives shape our understanding of who we are and what we are capable of. Reframing our personal stories to highlight resilience and growth empowers us to see ourselves as capable and resourceful. For example, instead of viewing a career setback as a failure, we might frame it as a turning point that led to new opportunities or deeper self-discovery. This shift in narrative not only strengthens our resilience but also inspires hope and motivation.

Connection is another essential element of resilience. Relationships provide support, perspective, and encouragement during difficult times. Reaching out to trusted friends, family members, or mentors fosters a sense of belonging and reminds us that we are not alone in our struggles. Sharing our experiences and listening to others' stories builds empathy and mutual strength, creating a network of resilience that extends beyond the individual.

Nature offers yet another source of resilience, providing a sense of calm and perspective that is difficult to find elsewhere. Spending time outdoors, whether walking through a forest, sitting by a river, or simply observing the changing seasons, reminds us of the cyclical nature of life. The Japanese practice of *shinrin-yoku*, or forest bathing, exemplifies this connection. By immersing ourselves in natural settings, we reconnect with the world's rhythms, finding solace and strength in its beauty and simplicity.

Resilience also benefits from acts of service and contribution. Helping others, whether through volunteering, mentoring, or small acts of kindness, shifts our focus outward and reinforces a sense of purpose. Service reminds us of our interconnectedness and the impact we can have on others, fostering a sense of empowerment and fulfillment. This outward focus often has the paradoxical effect of strengthening our own resilience, as it reinforces our capacity to create positive change even in the midst of challenges.

Finally, cultivating a sense of humor can lighten the emotional weight of difficult situations. Laughter, as research shows, reduces stress hormones, boosts mood, and strengthens social bonds. Finding moments of humor, even in challenging times, reminds us not to take ourselves too seriously and fosters a sense of resilience through playfulness and perspective.

These practices, though simple, have profound effects when integrated into daily life. They serve as anchors of stability, helping us navigate adversity with grace and strength. Resilience is not about avoiding difficulties but about facing them with courage, adaptability, and an unwavering belief in our capacity to grow. By incorporating these habits into our routines, we cultivate a reservoir of inner strength that sustains us, no matter what challenges arise.

CHAPTER 4: THE ART OF LETTING GO – RELEASING EMOTIONAL WEIGHT

Why Letting Go Is Hard

Letting go is one of the simplest yet most challenging acts we face in life. Whether it's the memory of a painful experience, the resentment of a past wrong, or the fear of an uncertain future, our minds have a way of clinging to emotional weights long after their usefulness has passed. This attachment often feels irrational—even counterproductive—yet it is deeply ingrained in our psychology and shaped by our experiences. To understand why letting go is so difficult, we must first explore the inner workings of the mind and the forces that tether us to what no longer serves us.

At the heart of this struggle lies a fundamental truth: the mind craves certainty. The unknown can feel threatening, and even painful memories offer a sense of familiarity that the unknown cannot provide. This craving for certainty stems from the brain's evolutionary design. The human brain is wired to seek patterns and predict outcomes, an ability that once ensured our survival in the face of predators and other dangers. However, this same mechanism now encourages us to hold onto familiar emotions, even when they cause suffering. Letting go, by contrast, requires stepping into uncertainty, trusting that release will bring healing—a leap that often feels daunting.

Attachment also stems from the stories we tell ourselves about our experiences. These narratives give meaning to our lives, shaping how we understand who we are and where we've been. While these stories can provide comfort and clarity, they can also trap us in cycles of pain and regret. For example, a person who identifies as "someone who was betrayed" might find it difficult to let go of resentment because doing so feels like abandoning a core aspect of their identity. This phenomenon, known as ego attachment, binds us to our emotional burdens, making it hard to separate who we are from what we've experienced.

The philosopher Søren Kierkegaard once wrote, "Life can only be understood backwards; but it must be lived forwards." This tension between reflection and progression highlights another reason why letting go is hard: the past holds a powerful grip on our present. We replay events in our minds, imagining how things could have been different, or we ruminate on the pain of what was lost. This backward focus often stems from a desire to make sense of our experiences, but it can also prevent us from moving forward. By clinging to the past, we deprive ourselves of the opportunity to fully engage with the present.

Another significant barrier to letting go is the fear of vulnerability. Emotional attachment often serves as a form of protection, a shield against the discomfort of uncertainty or the risk of being hurt again. For instance, holding onto anger might feel safer than confronting the sadness beneath it, just as replaying old grievances might feel more controllable than facing the ambiguity of the future. Letting go requires vulnerability—a willingness to confront our emotions honestly and to trust in the possibility of growth and healing.

Cultural and social influences also play a role in our difficulty with letting go. In a society that often equates success with control and self-sufficiency, the act of releasing control can feel counterintuitive. We are conditioned to "hold on" in various ways: to relationships, achievements, possessions, and even pain. Letting go, by contrast, is sometimes perceived as a form of weakness or failure, rather than the act of courage and strength that it truly is.

Historical and philosophical perspectives offer valuable insights into the human struggle with letting go. The Buddha, in his teachings on attachment, observed that clinging to impermanent things is a primary source of suffering. He likened this attachment to grasping a burning coal—an act that harms us even as we refuse to release it. Yet, the Buddha also emphasized that letting go is not about denying our emotions or experiences but about releasing our attachment to them. This distinction is crucial: letting go does not mean forgetting or invalidating the past; it means freeing ourselves from its grip so that we can move forward unencumbered.

Modern psychology reinforces this understanding. Therapists and researchers often describe the act of letting go as a process of acceptance—acknowledging our emotions without judgment and choosing not to let them define us. Practices like mindfulness and cognitive behavioral techniques can help individuals break the cycles of rumination and attachment, creating space for new perspectives and possibilities. For example, mindfulness encourages us to observe our thoughts and feelings as passing phenomena, like clouds drifting across the sky, rather than as permanent fixtures of our identity.

Despite its challenges, the act of letting go is profoundly liberating. It clears emotional clutter, creates space for growth, and opens the door to inner peace. Historical figures provide inspiring examples of this transformation. Nelson Mandela, after 27 years of imprisonment, chose to let go of bitterness and resentment, focusing instead on reconciliation and unity. His ability to release the weight of his suffering allowed him to become a powerful force for healing and change, both for himself and for his country.

Similarly, Maya Angelou, the renowned poet and civil rights activist, often spoke about the importance of releasing past pain. "You may not control all the events that happen to you," she said, "but you can decide not to be reduced by them." Angelou's words reflect the essence of letting go: reclaiming our power by choosing how we respond to our experiences.

Letting go is not a single act but a journey, one
that requires patience, self-compassion, and
practice. It begins with acknowledging the difficulty of the process and recognizing that attachment is a natural part of being human. From
there, we can begin to challenge the beliefs and
patterns that hold us back, replacing them with
new practices and perspectives that support our
growth.

Ultimately, the art of letting go is an act of courage. It is a decision to release what weighs us
down and to embrace the freedom that comes
with it. By letting go, we create space for new
beginnings, greater clarity, and a deeper connection to ourselves and the world around us.

Forgiveness as Freedom

Forgiveness is often described as a gift we give to
others, but its greatest power lies in the freedom
it grants ourselves. To forgive is not to excuse
wrongdoing or diminish the pain caused by it;
rather, it is to release the grip of resentment and
anger that binds us to the past. Forgiveness is an
act of liberation, a conscious choice to unburden
our hearts and reclaim our peace. While the

journey toward forgiveness can be challenging, it is also profoundly transformative, offering a path to healing and inner freedom.

At its core, forgiveness is a decision to let go of the emotional weight we carry in response to harm or betrayal. It is not about condoning harmful actions or forgetting the lessons they teach us; instead, it is about severing the emotional ties that keep us tethered to pain. This distinction is vital, as forgiveness often requires a nuanced balance between honoring our experiences and choosing not to let them define us.

The transformative power of forgiveness is illustrated in the story of Nelson Mandela, who endured 27 years of imprisonment under South Africa's apartheid regime. Upon his release, Mandela could have chosen bitterness and revenge, but he understood that such emotions would only perpetuate his suffering. Instead, he forgave those who had wronged him, focusing his energy on reconciliation and unity. "Resentment," Mandela said, "is like drinking poison and then hoping it will kill your enemies." His act of forgiveness not only freed him from the burden of anger but also set the stage for national healing.

Forgiveness is not a passive act but a courageous
and active process. It requires us to confront
our pain, acknowledge the depth of our hurt,
and make a conscious decision to let it go. This
process is often likened to climbing a mountain:
it can be steep and demanding, but the view
from the summit—a perspective unclouded by
resentment—is worth the effort. Along the way,
forgiveness challenges us to examine our beliefs about justice, fairness, and vulnerability,
pushing us to grow in ways we may not have
anticipated.

Psychology provides valuable insights into the
benefits of forgiveness. Studies have shown
that forgiving others is associated with lower
levels of stress, anxiety, and depression, as well
as improved physical health and relationships.
Dr. Fred Luskin, a leading researcher on forgiveness, describes it as a means of reclaiming
power over our lives. When we hold onto anger
or resentment, we give the offending person or
event control over our emotions. Forgiveness,
by contrast, restores our autonomy, allowing us
to choose peace over pain.

The act of forgiveness also aligns with teachings from spiritual and philosophical traditions. In Christianity, forgiveness is a central tenet, exemplified by Jesus's words on the cross: "Father, forgive them, for they know not what they do." This plea highlights the compassion inherent in forgiveness, recognizing that those who cause harm often act out of ignorance, fear, or their own unhealed wounds. Similarly, Buddhist teachings emphasize forgiveness as a means of breaking the cycle of suffering. The Dalai Lama, reflecting on the violence and exile he has faced, speaks of forgiveness as an act of self-preservation: "Holding onto anger is like grasping a hot coal with the intent of throwing it at someone else; you are the one who gets burned."

Forgiveness is not limited to forgiving others; it also involves forgiving ourselves. Self-forgiveness can be even more challenging, as it requires us to confront feelings of guilt, shame, or inadequacy. Yet, it is an essential aspect of healing. By acknowledging our imperfections and extending the same compassion to ourselves that we would offer a friend, we create space for growth and renewal. Maya Angelou captured this sentiment beautifully when she wrote, "Forgive yourself for not knowing what you didn't know before you learned it."

The path to forgiveness is deeply personal, and there is no one-size-fits-all approach. However, certain practices can support this journey. One such practice is empathy — the ability to see the situation from another's perspective. While empathy does not excuse harmful behavior, it can help us understand the motivations or circumstances that may have contributed to it. This understanding can soften the edges of anger and create room for compassion.

Another powerful practice is writing a forgiveness letter. In this exercise, we articulate our feelings — anger, sadness, disappointment — toward the person who hurt us. The goal is not to send the letter but to express and process our emotions fully, creating a sense of closure. For some, this practice may also involve writing a letter to themselves, offering forgiveness for past mistakes or regrets.

Meditation and mindfulness can also aid the process of forgiveness. A loving-kindness meditation, for example, involves silently repeating phrases of goodwill toward ourselves and others, including those who have hurt us. Phrases like "May you be happy, may you be healthy, may you be free from suffering" cultivate a sense of compassion and release. Over time, this practice can dissolve the barriers of anger and resentment, allowing forgiveness to take root.

The process of forgiveness is not linear, and it may take time to reach a place of genuine release. It is normal to revisit feelings of anger or hurt, especially when memories are triggered. However, each step toward forgiveness, no matter how small, contributes to the larger journey of healing. As we practice forgiveness, we gradually loosen the emotional chains that bind us, discovering a freedom that transcends the pain of the past.

Forgiveness does not mean forgetting; it means choosing not to let the past define our present. It is an act of courage and compassion, a decision to reclaim our power and embrace the peace that comes with release. By forgiving others and ourselves, we create space for healing, growth, and connection, transforming the burdens of the past into stepping stones for the future.

Acceptance Without Apathy

Acceptance is a profound act of strength, a willingness to acknowledge life as it is rather than
as we wish it to be. It is not resignation, nor is
it indifference; rather, it is a deliberate choice to
face reality with clarity and composure. Acceptance invites us to release resistance to circumstances beyond our control, but it does not ask
us to surrender our agency or aspirations. The
challenge lies in finding the balance between
accepting life's challenges and taking meaningful action—a balance that allows us to navigate
difficulties without succumbing to apathy.

At its essence, acceptance is about seeing clearly.
It is the ability to recognize what is within our
control and what is not, a distinction central to
the teachings of the Stoics. Epictetus, one of the
most renowned Stoic philosophers, emphasized
this principle: "Happiness and freedom begin
with a clear understanding of one principle:
some things are within our control, and some
things are not." By focusing our energy on what
we can influence—our thoughts, actions, and

attitudes—we free ourselves from the futile struggle against what lies beyond our reach.

However, acceptance is often misunderstood as passivity, a kind of fatalistic surrender. This misinterpretation leads to apathy, the belief that nothing can be changed and that our efforts are meaningless. True acceptance, by contrast, is dynamic and empowering. It allows us to engage with life's challenges more effectively because we are no longer wasting energy resisting the inevitable. Acceptance clears the mental clutter of "what if" and "if only," enabling us to act with greater focus and intention.

Consider the story of Helen Keller, who faced immense obstacles after losing her sight and hearing as a young child. Acceptance, for Keller, did not mean giving up on her dreams or resigning herself to her circumstances. Instead, it meant acknowledging her limitations while finding new ways to overcome them. Through determination and the support of her teacher, Anne Sullivan, Keller learned to communicate, write, and advocate for others with disabilities. Her life illustrates how acceptance can coexist with ambition, creating a foundation for resilience and impact.

Acceptance also requires us to confront our fears
and vulnerabilities. It is natural to resist difficult
emotions or circumstances, hoping that denial
will shield us from pain. Yet, this resistance
often amplifies our suffering, trapping us in
cycles of frustration and avoidance. Acceptance,
by contrast, invites us to sit with discomfort,
to allow our feelings and experiences to exist
without judgment. This act of acknowledgment,
while uncomfortable, is profoundly liberating.
As the psychologist Carl Rogers observed, "The
curious paradox is that when I accept myself
just as I am, then I can change."

Practicing acceptance does not mean abandoning hope or effort. It means starting from a place
of honesty, where we can assess our situation
with clear eyes and make choices grounded in
reality. This approach is evident in the philosophy of mindfulness, which emphasizes being
present with what is, without trying to change
or escape it. Mindfulness teaches us to observe
our thoughts and emotions with curiosity rather
than resistance, creating a space where acceptance and action can coexist.

One of the most striking examples of this balance comes from the life of Viktor Frankl, who survived the horrors of Nazi concentration camps. In his memoir, *Man's Search for Meaning*, Frankl described how accepting the harsh realities of his situation allowed him to focus on what he could control—his thoughts, attitudes, and sense of purpose. This perspective enabled him to endure unimaginable suffering and emerge with a renewed commitment to helping others find meaning in their own lives. Frankl's story demonstrates that acceptance is not about giving up; it is about grounding ourselves in the present so that we can move forward with purpose.

Strategies for practicing acceptance without apathy often begin with reframing our relationship to control. Rather than seeing acceptance as a loss of power, we can view it as an act of empowerment—an opportunity to focus on what truly matters. For example, in the face of a difficult relationship, acceptance might involve recognizing that we cannot change another person's behavior, but we can set boundaries and choose how we respond. This shift in perspec-

tive transforms acceptance from a passive state
to an active process, one that fosters both clarity
and agency.

Gratitude is another powerful tool for cultivating acceptance. By focusing on the aspects of
our lives that bring us joy or fulfillment, we can
counterbalance the challenges we face. Gratitude does not erase pain or difficulty, but it
provides a broader context, reminding us that
even in hardship, there is beauty and meaning
to be found. This practice encourages a mindset of abundance rather than scarcity, allowing
us to embrace life's complexities with greater
equanimity.

Acceptance also involves letting go of the need
for certainty. Life is inherently unpredictable,
and our attempts to control every outcome often
lead to frustration and anxiety. Embracing uncertainty requires trust—trust in ourselves, in
the process of life, and in our ability to adapt.
This trust is not blind optimism but a grounded confidence that we can navigate whatever
comes our way. As the Buddhist teacher Pema
Chödrön writes, "To be fully alive, fully human,
and completely awake is to be continually

thrown out of the nest. To live is to be willing to die over and over again."

Ultimately, acceptance without apathy is a practice of balance. It is the ability to hold two truths simultaneously: that some things cannot be changed, and that our response to them can. This balance allows us to engage with life authentically, embracing its joys and sorrows without losing ourselves in either. It is an act of courage, a willingness to face reality with open eyes and an open heart.

By cultivating acceptance, we free ourselves from the weight of resistance and open the door to possibility. Acceptance does not mean giving up; it means letting go of what holds us back so that we can move forward with strength and purpose. It is not the end of effort but the beginning of clarity, a path that leads to greater peace and resilience.

The Practice of Detachment

Detachment is not about withdrawing from life or becoming indifferent to its joys and challenges. Instead, it is a practice of releasing our attachment to outcomes, possessions, and even our own expectations. It is a deliberate choice to engage with the world fully while maintaining a sense of inner freedom. Through detachment, we learn to experience life without being consumed by it, finding peace amidst the inevitable changes and uncertainties of existence.

At its core, detachment is the recognition that clinging leads to suffering. This principle is central to Buddhist philosophy, which identifies attachment as one of the primary causes of human discontent. The Buddha taught that by craving permanence in an impermanent world, we set ourselves up for disappointment and pain. Detachment, therefore, is not about rejecting life but about embracing its impermanence with grace. It is a mindset that allows us to appreciate life's fleeting beauty without becoming ensnared by it.

The Stoics, too, understood the value of detachment. In their view, freedom lies in focusing on what is within our control and letting go of everything else. Epictetus, a prominent Stoic philosopher, advised, "Don't demand that things happen as you wish, but wish that they happen as they do, and you will go on well." This attitude of acceptance and detachment enables us to navigate life's challenges with resilience and composure, unburdened by unrealistic expectations or desires.

Detachment often begins with examining our relationship to control. Many of us hold tightly to the belief that we can shape every aspect of our lives, from the outcomes of our efforts to the behavior of those around us. While a certain degree of control is necessary and even healthy, an excessive need for control can lead to frustration and anxiety. Detachment invites us to loosen this grip, acknowledging that while we can influence some things, we cannot dictate every outcome. This shift in perspective is both humbling and liberating, reminding us to focus on what truly matters.

One practical way to cultivate detachment is through mindfulness. By bringing our attention to the present moment, we learn to observe our thoughts, emotions, and desires without becoming entangled in them. A simple mindfulness practice involves sitting quietly and noticing the flow of thoughts that arise. Rather than trying to suppress or analyze these thoughts, we simply let them come and go, like leaves floating down a stream. This exercise trains the mind to recognize the transient nature of our experiences, fostering a sense of inner calm and perspective.

Another aspect of detachment is releasing our attachment to material possessions. In a culture that often equates success with accumulation, this can be a challenging practice. However, detachment from material things does not mean rejecting them entirely. It means recognizing their temporary nature and refusing to let them define our worth or happiness. The Japanese concept of *wabi-sabi*, which celebrates the beauty of imperfection and impermanence, offers a valuable perspective on this practice. By appreciating the simple and the transient, we cultivate a sense of contentment that is not reliant on external circumstances.

Detachment also involves letting go of the need for approval from others. Many of us invest significant energy in seeking validation, shaping our actions and decisions to meet the expectations of those around us. While connection and feedback are important, over-reliance on external approval can erode our sense of self. Detachment from this need allows us to act authentically, guided by our own values rather than the shifting opinions of others. This practice requires courage, but it also fosters a deep sense of freedom and integrity.

Historical figures provide inspiring examples of detachment in action. Mahatma Gandhi, for instance, embodied the principle of detachment in his quest for India's independence. While deeply committed to his cause, Gandhi was not attached to specific outcomes or personal accolades. His focus was on living in alignment with his principles, trusting that his actions would contribute to a greater good. This sense of detachment allowed him to persevere through setbacks and challenges without losing sight of his purpose.

Similarly, Marcus Aurelius, the Roman emperor and Stoic philosopher, practiced detachment amidst the immense pressures of his role. In his meditations, he often reminded himself to remain grounded and not to be swayed by praise or criticism. "If you are distressed by anything external," he wrote, "the pain is not due to the thing itself but to your estimate of it; and this you have the power to revoke at any moment." Marcus's reflections highlight the power of detachment to create inner stability, even in the face of external turmoil.

The practice of detachment is not about abandoning relationships or passions; it is about approaching them with openness rather than attachment. In relationships, detachment means loving without clinging, allowing others the freedom to be themselves while maintaining our own sense of self. In our pursuits, it means striving with purpose and effort while accepting that outcomes are not entirely within our control. This balance enables us to engage deeply with life while preserving our peace of mind.

One powerful tool for cultivating detachment is journaling. Writing about our fears, desires, and attachments can help us identify the areas where we are holding on too tightly. By putting these thoughts into words, we create a sense of distance, allowing us to reflect on them with greater clarity. Questions such as "What am I afraid to lose?" or "How would I feel if this outcome didn't happen?" can uncover the roots of our attachments, offering insights that support the process of letting go.

Ultimately, detachment is a practice of freedom. It teaches us to release the burdens of clinging and craving, creating space for peace, joy, and connection. By embracing life's impermanence and focusing on what truly matters, we discover a sense of lightness and resilience that carries us through life's uncertainties. Detachment is not an act of withdrawal but of engagement—an invitation to live fully, unencumbered by the weight of attachment.

CHAPTER 5: NATURE'S EMBRACE – FINDING PEACE IN THE NATURAL WORLD

The Healing Power of Nature

Amid the noise and demands of modern life, the natural world offers a quiet sanctuary—a place where the body can rest, the mind can clear, and the spirit can rejuvenate. For centuries, poets, philosophers, and healers have extolled the restorative power of nature. Today, scientific research confirms what many have long intuitively known: spending time in nature has profound physical and mental health benefits. From reducing stress to boosting creativity, nature heals in ways that are as mysterious as they are undeniable.

The human connection to nature is deeply rooted in our biology. For most of human history, we lived in close relationship with the natural world, dependent on its rhythms and resources for survival. It is only in recent centuries, with the rise of industrialization and urbanization, that many of us have become distanced from these roots. Yet, our bodies and minds remain attuned to nature's cues. This connection is so intrinsic that scientists refer to it as *biophilia*, a term coined by biologist E.O. Wilson to describe humanity's innate affinity for the natural world.

One of the most well-documented benefits of spending time in nature is its ability to reduce stress. When we step into a forest or walk along a beach, our bodies begin to relax almost immediately. Heart rates slow, blood pressure drops, and levels of the stress hormone cortisol decrease. This phenomenon, known as the "relaxation response," is a physiological shift that counteracts the effects of chronic stress. A groundbreaking study conducted in Japan found that participants who engaged in *shinrin-yoku*, or forest bathing, experienced significant reductions in stress and improvements in immune function. The practice, which involves immersing oneself in the sights, sounds, and smells of a forest, has since become a cornerstone of preventative healthcare in Japan.

Nature's calming effects extend beyond the physiological to the psychological. Research has shown that time spent in green spaces enhances mood, reduces symptoms of anxiety and depression, and increases overall well-being. One reason for this is the way nature captures our attention. Unlike the constant demands of screens and urban environments, which drain our mental resources, natural settings engage us effortlessly. This type of gentle, involuntary attention—what psychologists call "soft fascination"—allows the mind to rest and recharge.

The healing power of nature is also reflected in its ability to boost creativity and focus. In a world where multitasking and information overload are the norms, stepping into a natural setting can help us clear mental clutter and regain clarity. A study conducted by researchers at the University of Utah found that participants who spent three days in the wilderness, disconnected from technology, showed a 50% improvement in creative problem-solving. This finding underscores the idea that nature not only restores but also inspires, offering a fertile ground for new ideas and perspectives.

Historical figures have long turned to nature for solace and insight. Henry David Thoreau's retreat to Walden Pond is perhaps one of the most famous examples. Seeking simplicity and clarity, Thoreau immersed himself in the natural world, drawing inspiration from its rhythms and beauty. In *Walden*, he wrote, "I went to the woods because I wished to live deliberately, to front only the essential facts of life, and see if I could not learn what it had to teach." His reflections continue to resonate, reminding us of nature's power to illuminate what truly matters.

Similarly, John Muir, the naturalist and founder of the Sierra Club, viewed nature as a source of spiritual renewal. He famously observed, "In every walk with nature, one receives far more than he seeks." Muir's advocacy for preserving wild spaces stemmed from his belief that nature is essential not only for physical health but also for emotional and spiritual well-being. His writings inspired generations to seek connection with the natural world, fostering a deeper appreciation for its healing power.

Modern practices like horticultural therapy and ecotherapy build on these insights, using nature as a therapeutic tool. Horticultural therapy, which involves gardening and interacting with plants, has been shown to reduce anxiety, improve mood, and enhance social connections. Similarly, ecotherapy, which encourages activities like nature walks and outdoor mindfulness exercises, leverages the restorative effects of natural environments to support mental health.

These practices highlight the versatility of nature as a healing resource, adaptable to diverse needs and circumstances.

The benefits of nature are not limited to those who can escape to remote wilderness areas. Even small doses of greenery—such as a walk in a local park, tending to a garden, or simply gazing at a tree through a window—can have a significant impact. Studies have shown that urban residents who live near green spaces report better mental health and higher life satisfaction than those who do not. This finding underscores the importance of integrating nature into our daily lives, even in the midst of busy, urban environments.

The connection between nature and health is also evident in its role in fostering a sense of awe and wonder. Standing beneath a towering redwood, watching a sunrise paint the sky with vibrant hues, or feeling the rhythm of waves against the shore reminds us of the vastness of the world and our place within it. This experience of awe has been linked to reduced stress, increased life satisfaction, and a greater sense of interconnectedness. It is as if, in the presence of nature's grandeur, our own worries shrink, and we are reminded of the beauty and resilience that surround us.

Ultimately, the healing power of nature lies not only in its ability to restore but also in its capacity to reconnect us—with ourselves, with others, and with the larger web of life. In a world that often feels fragmented and fast-paced, nature offers a counterbalance, a reminder of the simplicity and harmony that are always within reach. By making time to immerse ourselves in the natural world, we not only nurture our health but also cultivate a deeper sense of peace and purpose.

Lessons from the Natural World

Nature is an unparalleled teacher, offering profound lessons through its cycles, patterns, and quiet persistence. Observing the natural world invites us to reflect on the rhythms of life, fostering resilience, patience, and acceptance. It reminds us that just as seasons change and rivers flow, so too must we adapt and find harmony within life's inevitable fluctuations.

One of nature's most striking lessons is its cyclical nature. The changing seasons, for instance, demonstrate the impermanence of all things. Spring brings renewal and growth, summer offers abundance, autumn ushers in transition, and winter embodies rest and reflection. These cycles mirror the phases of our own lives, teaching us to embrace change rather than resist it. Just as winter prepares the ground for spring, moments of difficulty and stillness can pave the way for growth and renewal. This understanding fosters patience, allowing us to trust that challenges are not permanent but part of a larger process.

The Japanese concept of *mono no aware*, which translates to "the pathos of things," captures this sentiment beautifully. It emphasizes an appreciation for the fleeting nature of life, encouraging us to find beauty and meaning in impermanence. The cherry blossoms of Japan, which bloom briefly before falling, are a powerful symbol of this philosophy. Their ephemeral nature reminds us to cherish the present moment, knowing that it, too, will pass. By aligning ourselves with nature's rhythms, we cultivate acceptance and gratitude for the ever-changing tapestry of life.

Resilience is another key lesson offered by the natural world. Consider the strength of a tree bending in the wind. Its flexibility allows it to withstand storms that might uproot a more rigid structure. This ability to adapt and endure is echoed in the human experience. Life's challenges, like storms, test our strength and flexibility, requiring us to bend without breaking. Observing nature's resilience inspires us to approach adversity with a similar mindset, trusting in our capacity to recover and grow.

The resilience of nature is also evident in its capacity for regeneration. Forests recover after wildfires, rivers carve new paths after floods, and plants bloom again after harsh winters. These processes remind us that healing and renewal are not only possible but natural. The ability of the earth to restore itself encourages us to trust in our own resilience, even in the face of setbacks or losses. Just as the natural world adapts to change, so too can we find new ways to thrive in the aftermath of life's challenges.

Patience, often elusive in our fast-paced world,

is another virtue modeled by nature. The growth of a tree, the migration of a bird, or the formation of a canyon takes time, unfolding at its own pace. Nature does not rush, yet everything is accomplished. This principle is captured in the Taoist philosophy of *wu wei*, or "effortless action." It teaches that by aligning ourselves with the natural flow of life, rather than forcing outcomes, we can achieve more with less strain. Observing nature's patient progress encourages us to adopt a similar approach, trusting that growth and transformation cannot be hurried but must unfold in their own time.

The cycles of nature also teach us about letting go. Autumn leaves falling to the ground illustrate the necessity of release, clearing space for new growth. This act of surrender is a reminder that holding on too tightly to what no longer serves us can hinder our progress. By observing this natural process, we learn to let go with grace, trusting that release is not an end but a beginning.

One historical figure who drew deeply from nature's lessons was Ralph Waldo Emerson. As a leader of the Transcendentalist movement,

Emerson believed that nature was a mirror reflecting universal truths. In his essay "Nature," he wrote, "The creation of a thousand forests is in one acorn." This observation highlights nature's potential for growth and transformation, reminding us that even the smallest seeds—whether literal or metaphorical—contain the power to create something vast and enduring. Emerson's reflections encourage us to recognize and nurture the seeds of potential within ourselves and others.

Another profound teacher of nature's wisdom is the river. Flowing water exemplifies adaptability and persistence, carving through rock and shaping landscapes over time. A river does not resist obstacles; instead, it moves around them, finding the path of least resistance. This quality of flow is echoed in Stoic philosophy, which emphasizes the importance of focusing on what we can control and letting go of what we cannot. Just as a river adjusts its course without losing its direction, we, too, can navigate life's challenges with flexibility and purpose.

Nature's interdependence offers yet another valuable lesson. Every ecosystem is a web of relationships, where each element—plants, animals, soil, water—plays a role in maintaining balance. This interconnectedness reminds us that we are not separate from the world around us but part of a larger whole. Recognizing this connection fosters humility and compassion, encouraging us to support one another and care for the environment that sustains us.

Practically speaking, these lessons can be integrated into our daily lives through intentional observation and reflection. A walk through a park, a moment spent watching the clouds, or time tending to a garden can become opportunities to learn from nature's wisdom. By pausing to notice the resilience of a flower growing through concrete, the steady rhythm of waves on a shore, or the intricate patterns of a spider's web, we gain insights into our own lives. These small moments of connection remind us that nature's lessons are always available, waiting for us to slow down and listen.

Ultimately, the natural world teaches us that life is a balance of holding on and letting go, of growth and rest, of resilience and surrender. By observing and embracing these cycles, we

align ourselves with a wisdom far older and
deeper than our own. Nature's patterns offer a
framework for navigating life with grace and
clarity, reminding us that we are part of a larger
story—one of renewal, connection, and boundless possibility.

Simple Ways to Reconnect with Nature

Reconnecting with nature does not require
grand gestures or distant travel. The natural
world is all around us, waiting to be noticed,
appreciated, and engaged with. Whether you
live in a bustling city or a rural countryside,
there are countless ways to integrate nature into
your daily life. By making small, intentional
choices, we can restore our connection to the
earth, nurturing our physical, emotional, and
spiritual well-being.

One of the simplest and most accessible ways
to reconnect with nature is through mindful observation. Pausing to notice the details of your
surroundings—a tree swaying in the breeze,
the intricate patterns of a flower, or the changing colors of the sky—can ground you in the

present moment. This practice, often referred to as "nature mindfulness," invites us to engage all our senses. By listening to the rustle of leaves, feeling the warmth of sunlight on our skin, or inhaling the scent of freshly cut grass, we deepen our awareness and appreciation of the natural world. These moments of mindful observation act as a counterbalance to the distractions of modern life, offering a quiet space for reflection and renewal.

Gardening, whether on a small balcony or in a backyard, is another powerful way to reconnect with nature. The act of tending to plants fosters a sense of responsibility and care, reminding us of the interdependence between humans and the natural world. Gardening also engages us in the cycles of growth and renewal, teaching patience and providing a tangible connection to the earth. Even growing a single potted plant indoors can bring a touch of nature into your daily routine, serving as a reminder of life's resilience and beauty.

For those in urban settings, green spaces such as parks, community gardens, and tree-lined streets offer valuable opportunities to engage with nature. Taking a walk in a nearby park, sitting beneath a tree, or watching birds in flight can provide moments of tranquility and connection, even amidst the hustle of city life. Research shows that spending just 20 minutes in a green space can significantly reduce stress levels, underscoring the importance of seeking out these pockets of nature wherever they are available.

Water, too, holds a unique power to calm and restore. Whether it's the rhythmic sound of ocean waves, the gentle flow of a river, or the stillness of a lake, being near water can create a profound sense of peace. For those without access to natural water sources, fountains or small water features can replicate this soothing effect. Even listening to recordings of natural water sounds can evoke a sense of connection, reminding us of the elemental forces that sustain life.

Walking outdoors, particularly in natural settings, is a timeless way to engage with the environment. The rhythm of walking aligns with the rhythm of nature, creating a meditative state that clears the mind and restores the spirit. Historical figures such as Henry David Thoreau and John Muir extolled the virtues of walking as a means of connecting with the natural world. Muir, in particular, described walking as an act of reverence, writing, "In every walk with nature, one receives far more than he seeks." Whether it's a hike in the wilderness or a leisurely stroll through a neighborhood park, walking invites us to slow down, observe, and appreciate the world around us.

Bringing nature indoors is another effective way to maintain a connection to the environment. Houseplants, natural materials like wood and stone, and even nature-inspired artwork can transform living spaces into calming, restorative environments. Studies have shown that indoor plants improve air quality, boost mood, and enhance focus, making them a valuable addition to any home or workspace. By incorporating elements of nature into our interiors, we create a constant reminder of our bond with the natural world.

Creating rituals around nature can also deepen our connection. These rituals might include watching the sunrise or sunset, celebrating seasonal changes, or simply spending a few minutes each day sitting quietly outdoors. Rituals provide a sense of rhythm and intention, reinforcing our relationship with the earth and its cycles. They remind us to pause and honor the natural world, even in the midst of busy lives.

For families, nature offers a way to bond and create lasting memories. Activities such as planting a garden together, exploring a nearby trail, or simply observing wildlife in the backyard can instill a sense of wonder and appreciation in children. These shared experiences not only nurture connections within the family but also foster a lifelong respect for the environment.

Reconnecting with nature often leads to a ripple effect, inspiring us to take action to protect and preserve the environment. When we develop a personal relationship with the natural world, we become more attuned to its fragility and more motivated to care for it. This sense of stewardship enriches our connection, creating a cycle of reciprocity that benefits both ourselves and the planet.

Ultimately, the key to reconnecting with nature lies in simplicity and consistency. It is not about doing more but about being present with what is already around us. Nature invites us to slow down, to notice, and to engage—not as visitors but as participants in a larger ecosystem. Whether through a moment of quiet observation, a walk in the park, or the nurturing of a garden, these small acts bring us closer to the earth and to ourselves.

By integrating nature into our daily lives, we create a sanctuary of connection and peace, no matter where we are. The natural world is always there, waiting to be rediscovered, offering its quiet wisdom and boundless beauty to those who take the time to listen.

Finding Your Sanctuary

In a world that often feels chaotic and overwhelming, finding a personal sanctuary in nature offers more than just a reprieve—it becomes a source of strength, clarity, and renewal. A sanctuary is not merely a physical space; it is an experience, a feeling of connection and calm that allows us to pause, breathe, and realign with what truly matters. Whether it's a quiet grove in a forest, a sunlit corner of a park, or a familiar stretch of beach, your sanctuary is a place where the external noise fades, and the inner self finds peace.

The idea of sanctuary is rooted in human history. Ancient civilizations often revered sacred natural spaces—groves, mountains, rivers—as places of worship and reflection. These sites were seen as bridges between the human and the divine, offering not only spiritual connection but also solace and inspiration. While modern life may have distanced us from this reverence, the need for a personal haven remains as vital as ever. By creating or discovering our own sanctuaries, we honor this ancient impulse to find meaning and peace in the natural world.

Finding your sanctuary begins with reflection. What environments bring you a sense of calm? Where do you feel most at ease? For some, it might be a wide-open landscape that evokes freedom and possibility. For others, it could be a shaded nook in a dense forest, offering comfort and security. Pay attention to the places that draw you, and consider why they resonate with you. This process of introspection is as important as the sanctuary itself, guiding you toward spaces that align with your needs and emotions.

For Henry David Thoreau, his sanctuary was Walden Pond. In retreating to this tranquil body of water, Thoreau sought simplicity and solitude, immersing himself in nature to rediscover the essentials of life. His reflections, chronicled in *Walden,* reveal how deeply a sanctuary can shape our perspective and priorities. "I went to the woods because I wished to live deliberately," Thoreau wrote, emphasizing the power of stepping away from distractions to find clarity and purpose.

Your sanctuary need not be remote or grand. It could be a small garden, a favorite tree, or even a window with a view of the sky. What matters is the feeling it evokes—a sense of belonging, peace, and connection. In fact, accessibility is key to making your sanctuary a meaningful part of your life. The more easily you can visit it, the more likely it is to become a regular refuge in times of stress or reflection.

Once you've identified your sanctuary, take time to truly inhabit it. Leave your phone behind, or at least put it on silent, so you can be fully present. Notice the details of your surroundings: the way sunlight filters through leaves, the sound of birdsong or rustling grass, the texture of the ground beneath you. These sensory experiences ground you in the present moment, quieting the mental chatter and fostering a sense of mindfulness. Over time, the act of returning to your sanctuary becomes a ritual, reinforcing its role as a space for renewal and connection.

In cultivating your sanctuary, you may also find opportunities to personalize it. This could mean planting flowers or shrubs that bring you joy, placing a bench or chair in a shaded spot, or even marking the space with a small token of significance. These gestures deepen your relationship with the space, transforming it from a passive setting into an active part of your life. However, it's equally important to respect the natural integrity of the space, recognizing that your sanctuary exists within a larger ecosystem.

For many, the act of seeking a sanctuary becomes a metaphor for seeking inner peace. Nature's rhythms remind us of the cyclical nature of life—the ebb and flow of tides, the waxing and waning of the moon, the changing of seasons. These patterns offer perspective, showing us that just as the natural world undergoes periods of growth and rest, so too must we allow ourselves moments of stillness and reflection. In this way, the sanctuary becomes not only a physical space but also a mental and emotional state, one that we can carry with us even after leaving the natural world.

John Muir, the great naturalist, often wrote about his experiences in the wilderness as moments of profound spiritual connection. For Muir, nature itself was a cathedral, a sanctuary where he felt closest to the divine. "In God's wildness lies the hope of the world," he declared, expressing the belief that nature's beauty and majesty could heal and inspire the human soul. Muir's writings remind us that sanctuaries are not just places of retreat but also places of revelation, where we rediscover our connection to the larger web of life.

In practical terms, creating a sanctuary in nature also involves making it a priority. Modern life is filled with competing demands, and it's easy to let time in nature slip down the list of priorities. Yet, even brief visits to your sanctuary—whether for a few minutes or a few hours—can have a profound impact. Scheduling regular time to immerse yourself in this space reinforces its importance and ensures that it remains a consistent source of peace and grounding.

For those unable to access natural sanctuaries regularly, bringing elements of nature into your home or workspace can serve as a substitute. Houseplants, natural light, and even photographs of landscapes can evoke the calming essence of the outdoors. These small touches remind us of the sanctuary's presence, even when we cannot physically be there.

Ultimately, your sanctuary is more than a place; it is a relationship. It is a space that grows and evolves with you, offering solace in moments of difficulty and celebration in times of joy. By finding and nurturing this connection, you cultivate a wellspring of inner peace that supports you in navigating the complexities of life. Whether it's a hidden corner of a bustling city or a vast expanse of wilderness, your sanctuary awaits—a quiet refuge where you can recharge, reflect, and reconnect with the essence of who you are.

CHAPTER 6: THE BALANCE BLUEPRINT – HARMONIZING LIFE'S DEMANDS

The Myth of Perfect Balance

Balance is a word that evokes a sense of serenity and control, a vision of life's demands distributed neatly across the scales of time and energy. It's a concept that countless self-help books and motivational talks have encouraged us to strive for, promising fulfillment if only we could balance work, relationships, health, and personal growth. But despite our best efforts, perfect balance remains elusive, a goal that always seems just out of reach. This is because the very notion of perfect balance is a myth—a construct that oversimplifies the complexities of life and sets us up for unnecessary guilt and frustration.

Life, by its very nature, is dynamic and unpredictable. It ebbs and flows, presenting us with shifting priorities, unexpected challenges, and opportunities that require us to adapt. The pursuit of perfect balance assumes that life's demands are static and that we can distribute our attention evenly across all areas at all times. In reality, attempting to achieve this kind of balance often leads to feelings of inadequacy when the inevitable happens: one area of life temporarily takes precedence over another. This is not a failure; it is the rhythm of existence.

The ancient Chinese philosophy of Taoism offers a more nuanced perspective on balance. Central to Taoism is the concept of *wu wei*, or "effortless action," which emphasizes harmony with the natural flow of life rather than rigid control. In this view, balance is not about maintaining perfect equilibrium but about navigating life's shifts with grace and adaptability. Just as a river flows around obstacles without losing its direction, we are called to adjust to life's demands without clinging to the idea of perfection.

One of the most pervasive challenges in modern life is the expectation to "have it all." This ideal suggests that we can simultaneously excel in every domain—career, family, health, hobbies—without compromise. While ambition and drive are valuable, the notion of having it all at once is both unrealistic and unsustainable. Instead, a more realistic approach acknowledges that different seasons of life call for different priorities. There may be times when work demands more of our energy, while at other times, relationships or personal growth take center stage. Recognizing and accepting these shifts allows us to focus on what matters most in the moment, rather than striving for an unattainable ideal.

The myth of perfect balance is further complicated by societal pressures and the influence of social media. In an era where curated images of seemingly perfect lives flood our screens, it's easy to fall into the trap of comparison. We see snapshots of others excelling in areas where we feel we are falling short, creating a false sense of inadequacy. Yet, these glimpses rarely reflect the full picture. Behind every success story is a complex narrative of choices, sacrifices, and trade-offs. By letting go of comparisons, we can focus on crafting a life that aligns with our unique values and circumstances.

Philosophers and thought leaders throughout history have challenged the notion of balance as a static ideal. The Roman Stoic Seneca, for example, emphasized the importance of prioritizing what truly matters. In his letters, he wrote, "It is not that we have a short time to live, but that we waste a lot of it." Seneca's words remind us that balance is not about doing everything but about doing the right things. By aligning our actions with our core values, we can create a sense of harmony that feels authentic, even if it doesn't conform to conventional notions of balance.

One way to move beyond the myth of perfect balance is to reframe it as a dynamic process rather than a fixed state. Instead of striving for equal distribution of time and energy, we can aim for a sense of alignment—where our actions reflect our priorities and values. This approach allows for flexibility and acknowledges that life's demands will vary. For instance, during a major work project, personal hobbies may take a temporary backseat. Similarly, during a family crisis, career ambitions may momentarily recede. Rather than viewing these shifts as imbalances, we can see them as necessary adjustments that reflect the realities of life.

Practical strategies for embracing this dynamic approach include setting clear priorities, practicing self-compassion, and periodically reassessing our commitments. Setting priorities involves identifying what truly matters in the present moment and dedicating our energy accordingly. This requires honest self-reflection and the courage to say no to tasks or obligations that do not align with our goals. Self-compassion, on the other hand, helps us navigate the inevitable trade-offs with kindness rather than self-criticism. It reminds us that we are human, capable of doing many things but not all things simultaneously.

Periodic reassessment is also essential. Just as seasons change, so do our priorities and capacities. Taking time to evaluate where we are and where we want to be allows us to adjust our focus and resources as needed. This practice of recalibration ensures that our lives remain aligned with our values, even as circumstances evolve.

The concept of balance as a dynamic process is beautifully illustrated in the metaphor of a tightrope walker. A tightrope walker does not achieve balance by remaining perfectly still; instead, they constantly make small adjustments, shifting their weight and position to maintain stability. Similarly, our lives require ongoing adjustments to navigate the complexities of work, relationships, and personal growth. Balance, in this sense, is not a destination but an ongoing journey.

Ultimately, letting go of the myth of perfect balance is an act of liberation. It frees us from the unrealistic expectation to excel in all areas at once and allows us to focus on what truly matters. By embracing balance as a fluid, ever-changing process, we can approach life with greater flexibility, resilience, and peace of mind. In doing so, we create a blueprint for harmony that reflects the unique contours of our lives—a balance that is not perfect but perfectly ours.

Creating Your Life Compass

In the journey to harmonize life's demands, having a clear sense of direction is essential. Without it, we risk drifting aimlessly, pulled by the tides of external expectations and urgent demands. A life compass serves as this guiding instrument, helping us navigate the complexities of modern life with purpose and clarity. Unlike a traditional compass that points north, a life compass aligns us with our core values, ensuring that our actions and decisions reflect what truly matters.

The foundation of a life compass lies in identifying your core values—the principles and beliefs that define who you are and what you stand for. These values act as the anchor points of your compass, guiding you through uncertainty and keeping you grounded amidst competing priorities. For some, these values may include family, integrity, creativity, or personal growth. For others, they might emphasize adventure, service, or faith. The key is to uncover the values that resonate most deeply with you, forming the bedrock of your decisions and aspirations.

The process of identifying core values requires introspection and honesty. Begin by reflecting on moments in your life when you felt deeply fulfilled or proud. What was happening in those moments? What values were being honored? Conversely, think about times of conflict or dissatisfaction. What values were being compromised or ignored? These reflections provide valuable insights into the principles that shape your sense of purpose and well-being.

Philosophers throughout history have emphasized the importance of living in alignment with one's values. Aristotle, in his teachings on virtue ethics, argued that the good life is achieved through living virtuously—acting in accordance with one's highest principles. He described this state as *eudaimonia*, often translated as "flourishing" or "living well." For Aristotle, flourishing was not about external success but about cultivating inner excellence and integrity. This philosophy remains profoundly relevant today, reminding us that true fulfillment comes from living a life consistent with our values.

Once your core values are clear, the next step is to align your daily activities with them. This alignment is the essence of creating a life compass—it transforms abstract principles into tangible actions. For example, if one of your core values is family, consider how your daily schedule reflects that priority. Are you dedicating quality time to your loved ones, or is work consistently taking precedence? If creativity is a central value, how often do you make space for creative pursuits? This alignment process is not about perfection but about intentionality—ensuring that your actions support your values rather than undermine them.

A practical framework for aligning your life with your values is the practice of life auditing. This involves evaluating how you currently spend your time, energy, and resources, and comparing it to your ideal vision. Begin by tracking your activities for a week, noting how much time you devote to work, relationships, self-care, hobbies, and other commitments. Then, reflect on how well these activities align with your core values. Are there areas where you feel out of sync? Are there opportunities to adjust your priorities or redistribute your time? This exercise provides a clear picture of where you are and where you want to go, allowing you to recalibrate your compass as needed.

Historical figures offer inspiring examples of living in alignment with one's values. Consider Mahatma Gandhi, whose life was a testament to his principles of nonviolence, truth, and simplicity. Gandhi's commitment to these values guided his actions, from leading India's independence movement to choosing a lifestyle of austerity and self-discipline. His life compass was so firmly rooted in his values that even in the face of immense challenges, he remained unwavering in his mission. Gandhi's example underscores the power of a clear compass to provide strength and direction, even in the most turbulent times.

Another powerful example is Viktor Frankl, the psychiatrist and Holocaust survivor who found meaning amidst unimaginable suffering. In his seminal work, *Man's Search for Meaning*, Frankl described how his sense of purpose—rooted in his values of hope, love, and service—sustained him during his imprisonment in Nazi concentration camps. Frankl's experience illustrates that even in the darkest moments, a life compass can provide a sense of orientation, helping us navigate adversity with resilience and hope.

Creating your life compass also involves embracing flexibility. Just as a physical compass adjusts to magnetic fields, your life compass must adapt to changing circumstances. Values may remain constant, but the way we honor them often evolves. For instance, a value of service might initially manifest as a career in teaching but later take the form of volunteering or mentoring. By remaining open to these shifts, we ensure that our compass continues to guide us effectively.

It's also important to acknowledge that alignment with one's values is not a one-time achievement but an ongoing practice. Life is filled with distractions and competing demands, and it's natural to veer off course from time to time. The key is to regularly revisit your values and recalibrate your compass, ensuring that your actions remain aligned with your principles. This practice of realignment fosters a sense of authenticity and integrity, allowing you to move through life with confidence and purpose.

One practical tool for maintaining alignment is the use of a personal mission statement. A mission statement distills your core values and aspirations into a concise declaration of intent. For example, a mission statement might read, "To live with compassion, creativity, and courage, and to inspire others to do the same." Writing and revisiting your mission statement serves as a reminder of your guiding principles, reinforcing your commitment to living in alignment with your values.

Ultimately, creating your life compass is an act of empowerment. It shifts the focus from external expectations to internal clarity, allowing you to navigate life on your terms. With a well-defined compass, you can approach decisions with confidence, knowing that your choices reflect what truly matters to you. This alignment brings a sense of harmony and fulfillment, transforming life's demands into opportunities for growth and expression.

In a world filled with distractions and pressures, a life compass offers a steady anchor—a reminder of who you are and where you are going. By identifying your core values and aligning your actions with them, you create a blueprint for a meaningful and authentic life. Your compass becomes not only a guide but also a source of strength, illuminating the path to greater balance and purpose.

Setting Boundaries with Confidence

In a world where demands on our time and energy seem endless, setting boundaries is an essential act of self-preservation and self-respect. Boundaries are not walls that isolate us from others but bridges that define the space where mutual respect and understanding can flourish. They allow us to protect our well-being, focus on what truly matters, and navigate life's complexities with clarity and intention. Yet, many of us struggle to set and maintain boundaries, fearing rejection, conflict, or the guilt of saying no. The key to overcoming these challenges lies in cultivating the confidence to assert our needs and prioritize our values.

At its core, boundary-setting is an exercise in self-awareness. It begins with understanding your limits—what you can give without compromising your well-being, and what you need to maintain your energy and peace of mind. These limits are deeply personal, shaped by your values, responsibilities, and unique circumstances. Identifying them requires honest reflection. What drains you? What energizes you? Where do you feel resentment or frustration? These emotions often signal areas where boundaries are needed or have been crossed.

Once you've identified your limits, the next step is to communicate them clearly and confidently. This can feel daunting, especially if you're unaccustomed to asserting yourself. However, framing boundaries as expressions of respect— for both yourself and others—can help shift your perspective. By setting boundaries, you're not only honoring your needs but also creating a foundation for healthier, more authentic relationships. As the author and researcher Brené Brown puts it, "Clear is kind. Unclear is unkind." Clarity in communication fosters understanding and reduces the likelihood of misunderstandings or resentment.

Saying no is perhaps one of the most challenging aspects of boundary-setting, yet it is also one of the most powerful. The fear of disappointing others often leads us to overcommit, stretching ourselves too thin and compromising our priorities. But saying no is not an act of rejection; it is an affirmation of your values and capacities. By saying no to what doesn't align with your priorities, you create space to say yes to what does. Consider the words of Warren Buffett, who attributed much of his success to his ability to say no: "The difference between successful people and really successful people is that really successful people say no to almost everything."

The act of saying no becomes easier when we recognize that it is not our responsibility to meet every expectation or solve every problem. This requires letting go of the need for external validation and embracing the reality that we cannot

please everyone. It also involves reframing no
as an act of integrity rather than selfishness. By
declining commitments that don't serve us, we
are better able to show up fully for the commitments that do.

Delegation is another vital aspect of boundary-setting, particularly in professional and col-
laborative contexts. Many of us hesitate to dele-
gate, either out of fear of burdening others or a
belief that we must do everything ourselves. Yet,
delegation is not a sign of weakness but of trust
and leadership. It acknowledges that we cannot
and should not shoulder every responsibility
alone. Effective delegation involves identifying
tasks that can be shared or reassigned, clearly communicating expectations, and trusting
others to carry them out. This practice not only
lightens your load but also empowers those
around you to contribute and grow.

Protecting personal time is perhaps the most
tangible way to enforce boundaries. In a culture
that often glorifies busyness, carving out time
for rest, reflection, and self-care can feel like an
act of rebellion. Yet, it is precisely this time that
sustains us, allowing us to recharge and show

up fully in all areas of life. Scheduling personal time—whether it's an evening walk, a weekend without obligations, or simply 15 minutes of solitude each day—is an act of prioritizing your well-being. Treat this time as non-negotiable, just as you would a meeting or appointment. By doing so, you signal to yourself and others that your well-being matters.

Historical figures offer powerful examples of the importance of boundaries in achieving balance and clarity. Mahatma Gandhi, despite leading a monumental movement for India's independence, was known for his unwavering commitment to daily practices of rest and reflection. Gandhi's adherence to these routines—spinning thread, writing letters, and meditating—allowed him to maintain his focus and energy amidst immense demands. His example illustrates that even in the busiest of lives, boundaries are essential for sustaining purpose and effectiveness.

Similarly, Eleanor Roosevelt demonstrated the power of setting boundaries in her role as First Lady of the United States. Known for her tireless advocacy and public engagement, Roosevelt was also deliberate about carving out time for solitude and reflection. She once said, "The future belongs to those who believe in the beauty of their dreams," underscoring the importance of protecting space for creativity and vision amidst a whirlwind of responsibilities.

Setting boundaries also requires resilience, as not everyone will immediately understand or respect them. There may be pushback, particularly from those who have benefited from your lack of boundaries in the past. This is where confidence and consistency become crucial. Remember that your boundaries are not about controlling others but about taking responsibility for your own well-being. Over time, as you uphold your boundaries with clarity and kindness, others will begin to adjust and respect them.

Practicing boundary-setting can feel uncomfortable at first, especially if you're accustomed to prioritizing others' needs over your own. Start small, setting boundaries in low-stakes situations to build confidence. For example, you might decline an invitation to an event that doesn't interest you or let a colleague know that you need uninterrupted time to focus on a project. Celebrate these small victories, recognizing that each boundary you set is a step toward greater balance and authenticity.

Ultimately, boundaries are acts of love—love for yourself and for those around you. They create a framework for healthy relationships, meaningful work, and sustainable living. By setting boundaries with confidence, you honor your needs, protect your energy, and align your life with your values. In doing so, you create space for what truly matters, transforming overwhelm into harmony and intention.

The Rhythms of Life

Life, much like nature, unfolds in rhythms and cycles. From the changing of the seasons to the ebb and flow of the tides, the world around us is a symphony of movement, rest, and renewal. Yet, modern life often pushes us to ignore these natural rhythms, favoring constant activity over balance. By realigning ourselves with life's inherent cycles, we can cultivate harmony, resilience, and a deeper sense of purpose.

The concept of seasonal living—adapting our

actions and priorities to the natural rhythms of life—has roots in many ancient traditions. In agrarian societies, the seasons dictated the flow of daily life. Spring brought planting, summer demanded labor, autumn offered harvest, and winter invited rest. These cycles were not merely practical but deeply symbolic, reflecting the natural balance of work and renewal. While most of us no longer rely on the seasons for our survival, their wisdom remains relevant. Embracing the rhythms of life reminds us that rest is as vital as action, and that growth often requires periods of dormancy.

In modern contexts, seasonal living can take many forms. It might mean aligning your energy with the seasons of the year, allowing yourself to slow down and reflect in winter or to embrace creativity and connection in spring. It could also involve recognizing the rhythms within a single day—acknowledging when you are most alert and productive versus when you need rest. Honoring these cycles helps us avoid burnout and fosters greater efficiency and well-being.

The Stoics understood the importance of accepting life's cycles. Marcus Aurelius, in his *Medita-*

tions, wrote, "Observe constantly that all things take place by change, and accustom yourself to consider that the nature of the Universe loves nothing so much as to change the things that are and to make new things like them." His reflections remind us that change and rhythm are intrinsic to existence, and that by embracing them, we can navigate life's fluctuations with grace.

One practical way to align with life's rhythms is through mindfulness. By paying attention to your energy levels, emotions, and needs, you can begin to notice patterns. For instance, you might observe that you feel more introspective during certain times of the year or more energized at specific times of the day. These observations can inform how you structure your time, allowing you to work with your natural rhythms rather than against them.

This practice is particularly important in a culture that often glorifies productivity at the expense of rest. Rest, however, is not a luxury — it is a fundamental part of the rhythm of life. Consider the example of musicians: the pauses between notes are as integral to the melody as the notes themselves. Similarly, the pauses in our lives—the moments of stillness and reflection—are essential for maintaining balance and creativity. By honoring the need for rest, we create space for renewal and inspiration.

Nature offers countless examples of the wisdom of rhythm and flow. The tides, for instance, illustrate the balance of giving and receiving. High tide brings abundance, while low tide creates space. This cyclical movement mirrors the ebb and flow of human energy and emotion. Just as the ocean cannot remain at high tide indefinitely, we, too, must allow ourselves periods of retreat and restoration. Ignoring this need leads to exhaustion and imbalance, while embracing it fosters sustainability and growth.

The rhythms of life also teach us patience. Growth, whether in nature or in our own lives, cannot be rushed. A tree does not bear fruit immediately after it is planted; it requires time, care, and the right conditions. Similarly, our goals and aspirations often unfold in their own time. By aligning with the natural pace of progress, we reduce frustration and cultivate a sense of trust in the process.

Historical figures offer inspiring examples of living in harmony with life's rhythms. Leonardo da Vinci, known for his prolific creativity, also understood the value of stepping back. He often paused his work for extended periods, allowing ideas to gestate before returning with renewed clarity. This cyclical approach to creation reflects the rhythm of inspiration and rest, a balance that enabled da Vinci to produce some of history's most remarkable works.

Incorporating seasonal living into daily life does not require drastic changes. It begins with small, intentional shifts—recognizing when you need to rest, when to push forward, and when to reflect. For example, you might establish a morning routine that aligns with your natural energy levels, dedicating your most focused hours to meaningful work. Alternatively, you might create rituals to mark transitions, such as lighting a candle at the end of the workday to signal a shift from activity to rest.

Another way to embrace life's rhythms is to practice gratitude for each season, both literal and metaphorical. Just as autumn's beauty lies

in its transition, the challenges and changes in
our lives often hold hidden gifts. By appreciating each phase for what it offers, we cultivate a
sense of presence and acceptance.

The rhythms of life also invite us to consider
the long view. In a society that prizes instant re-
sults, it can be difficult to remember that growth
and transformation often occur over years, not
days. Nature reminds us of this truth through
its cycles of regeneration. A forest devastated
by fire, for instance, takes decades to recover
fully, yet the process is no less beautiful for its
slowness. Similarly, our own journeys require
patience and perseverance. By aligning with
these rhythms, we find solace in the understanding that progress, however gradual, is
always unfolding.

Ultimately, the rhythms of life teach us to embrace both action and stillness, growth and rest,
effort and surrender. By honoring these cycles,
we create a blueprint for harmony that reflects
the natural balance of the world around us. Life,
like a well-composed symphony, thrives on the
interplay of contrasts. In learning to navigate its
rhythms, we discover a deeper sense of peace

and purpose—a life not of relentless striving but of graceful flow.

CHAPTER 7: TIMELESS PRACTICES – RITUALS FOR INNER CALM

The Power of Ritual

In the whirl of modern life, where demands are relentless and distractions abound, rituals offer a steady anchor, a moment of pause in the chaos. They are the thread that weaves meaning and stability into our days, grounding us amidst uncertainty. Rituals are not confined to grand ceremonies or religious traditions; they can be as simple as lighting a candle at dusk, sipping tea in quiet reflection, or journaling at the start of a new day. What makes these acts powerful is their intentionality—the deliberate choice to engage in a practice that fosters connection, clarity, and calm.

The human inclination toward ritual is ancient and universal. Across cultures and centuries, rituals have marked transitions, celebrated milestones, and offered solace in times of difficulty. From the quiet meditations of Zen monks to the rhythmic chanting of Gregorian monks, rituals have long been a means of centering the mind and spirit. This enduring tradition reflects a fundamental truth: rituals help us make sense of the world and our place within it.

At their core, rituals are a form of mindfulness in action. By focusing our attention on a single task or moment, we create a sense of presence that counteracts the fragmented nature of daily life. This presence fosters a state of inner calm, allowing us to approach challenges with greater clarity and resilience. Research supports this idea, showing that rituals can reduce stress, enhance focus, and improve emotional well-being. The deliberate and repetitive nature of rituals provides a sense of predictability and control, qualities that are especially comforting in times of uncertainty.

One profound example of the power of ritual comes from the Japanese tea ceremony, or *chanoyu*. Rooted in Zen philosophy, this practice transforms the simple act of making and drinking tea into a meditative experience. Every movement in the ceremony, from the arrangement of utensils to the pouring of water, is performed with precision and mindfulness. Participants are encouraged to savor each moment, fully immersing themselves in the process. The tea ceremony exemplifies how even the most ordinary tasks can be elevated into rituals that promote peace and presence.

Similarly, the Stoics of ancient Rome recognized the value of rituals in cultivating inner strength and focus. Marcus Aurelius, the philosopher-emperor, often began his day with a ritual of reflection, reminding himself of his values and priorities. In his *Meditations*, he wrote, "When you arise in the morning, think of what a privilege it is to be alive—to think, to enjoy, to love." This simple yet intentional practice helped Aurelius navigate the challenges of leadership with composure and purpose.

The power of ritual lies not only in its ability to calm the mind but also in its capacity to imbue life with meaning. In a world that often feels rushed and transactional, rituals invite us to slow down and reconnect with what matters most. They serve as a bridge between the mundane and the sacred, transforming everyday moments into opportunities for gratitude and reflection.

One of the most significant benefits of rituals is their ability to create structure in our lives. This structure provides a sense of stability, especially during periods of upheaval or change.

For example, a morning ritual can set a positive tone for the day, while an evening ritual can signal a transition from work to rest. Over time, these practices become a source of comfort and strength, reminding us that even amidst chaos, there are moments we can control.

Creating a personal ritual does not require elaborate preparations or extensive time commitments. The most impactful rituals are often the simplest, tailored to individual needs and preferences. What matters is the intention behind the practice—the conscious decision to carve out a moment of peace and presence in the midst of life's demands. This intention transforms ordinary acts into powerful tools for cultivating inner calm.

Consider the act of lighting a candle. On the surface, it may seem insignificant, but as a ritual, it can carry profound meaning. The flame becomes a symbol of light and hope, a focal point for meditation or prayer. In the soft glow of the candlelight, the mind quiets, and the spirit finds solace. This is the essence of ritual: the transformation of the ordinary into the extraordinary through intention and awareness.

Historical figures have often relied on rituals to navigate the challenges of their lives. Mahatma Gandhi, for instance, practiced daily spinning as a form of meditation and discipline. For Gandhi, spinning was not only a political statement but also a personal ritual that grounded him in his principles of simplicity and self-reliance. This repetitive, intentional act provided a sense of focus and calm, allowing him to maintain clarity amidst the pressures of his mission.

Incorporating rituals into modern life offers a way to counterbalance the pace and complexity of the digital age. With so much competing for our attention, rituals provide a way to reclaim moments of stillness and meaning. They remind us to pause, breathe, and reconnect with ourselves and the world around us.

To begin integrating rituals into your life, start with small, intentional acts that align with your values and needs. It might be as simple as taking a few deep breaths before starting your day, writing down three things you're grateful for each evening, or pausing to enjoy a cup of tea without distractions. Over time, these practices become anchors—steady points of calm that help you navigate the currents of life with greater ease.

Ultimately, rituals are a testament to the human capacity for finding beauty and meaning in the simplest of acts. They are reminders that amidst the noise and haste, there is always an opportunity to pause and return to ourselves. By embracing the power of ritual, we create a sanctuary within—a space of calm and clarity that sustains us through life's ever-changing landscape.

Breathwork and Relaxation Techniques

The breath is a bridge between the conscious and unconscious mind, a constant yet often overlooked rhythm that sustains us. It is the first act we perform upon entering the world and the last as we leave it. Between those two moments, the way we breathe reflects our physical, emotional, and mental states. Shallow, rapid breaths often signal stress or anxiety, while deep, steady breaths evoke calm and presence. By learning to harness the power of the breath, we can create a profound sense of inner peace and resilience.

Ancient traditions have long recognized the significance of breath in cultivating balance and well-being. In yoga, *pranayama*, or breath control, is one of the core practices, believed to regulate the flow of life force energy, or *prana*. Similarly, Buddhist meditation often incorporates mindful breathing as a way to anchor the mind and calm the body. These practices remind us that the breath is more than a physiological process; it is a tool for transformation, a gateway to the present moment.

Modern science has begun to affirm what these ancient traditions have known for centuries. Research shows that intentional breathwork can reduce stress, lower blood pressure, improve focus, and even enhance emotional regulation. When we breathe deeply and deliberately, the parasympathetic nervous system—the body's "rest and digest" mode—is activated, counteracting the fight-or-flight response triggered by stress. This physiological shift creates a sense of calm, clarity, and control.

One of the simplest yet most effective breathwork techniques is diaphragmatic breathing, often referred to as belly breathing. Unlike shallow chest breathing, which is common during stress, diaphragmatic breathing engages the diaphragm, allowing the lungs to expand fully. This method not only increases oxygen intake but also sends a signal to the brain that it is safe to relax. To practice diaphragmatic breathing, sit or lie in a comfortable position, place one hand on your chest and the other on your abdomen, and focus on directing each inhale into your belly, feeling it rise with each breath. As you exhale, let your belly fall naturally, releasing tension.

Another powerful technique is the 4-7-8 breathing method, popularized by Dr. Andrew Weil. This practice involves inhaling through the nose for four counts, holding the breath for seven counts, and exhaling through the mouth for eight counts. The extended exhale activates the parasympathetic nervous system, creating a calming effect that can be particularly helpful during moments of anxiety or before sleep. This rhythmic breathing pattern mirrors the slow, steady tempo of a calm heartbeat, encouraging both physical and emotional relaxation.

For those seeking to deepen their connection to the breath, alternate nostril breathing, or *nadi shodhana*, is a traditional yogic practice that balances the body's energy channels. This technique involves using the thumb and ring finger to alternately close each nostril while breathing in and out. The process is both calming and centering, believed to harmonize the left and right hemispheres of the brain. Practitioners often find that this method sharpens focus and fosters a sense of equilibrium.

Breathwork is not limited to formal practices; it can be seamlessly integrated into daily life. Pausing to take a few deep breaths before a challenging conversation, during a stressful commute, or at the start of a busy day can shift your state of mind and enhance your ability to navigate the situation. These micro-moments of mindful breathing act as anchors, grounding you in the present and creating space between stimulus and response.

Historical figures have often turned to the breath as a source of strength and calm. The Roman emperor and Stoic philosopher Marcus Aurelius likely practiced mindful breathing as part of his daily reflections. In his *Meditations*, he wrote, "You have power over your mind—not outside events. Realize this, and you will find strength." This sentiment underscores the role of breath in reclaiming control over one's inner state, even amidst external chaos.

Similarly, the renowned monk Thich Nhat Hanh has spoken extensively about the role of mindful breathing in achieving inner peace. "Feelings come and go like clouds in a windy sky. Conscious breathing is my anchor," he wrote, highlighting how the breath serves as a constant amidst the ever-changing landscape of thoughts and emotions. His teachings emphasize the simplicity and accessibility of mindful breathing, a practice that anyone can adopt regardless of their circumstances.

The benefits of breathwork extend beyond moments of stress; they also enhance long-term well-being. Regular practice builds resilience, teaching the body and mind to recover more quickly from challenges. It creates a sense of spaciousness within, a pause that allows us to respond to life's demands with intention rather

than reaction. Over time, these practices cultivate a deep reservoir of calm that we can draw
upon whenever needed.

Relaxation techniques often complement breathwork, amplifying its effects. Progressive muscle
relaxation, for instance, involves tensing and
then slowly releasing different muscle groups,
starting from the toes and moving upward. This
practice not only eases physical tension but also
enhances awareness of the mind-body connection. Guided imagery, another relaxation technique, uses visualization to transport the mind
to a peaceful setting, such as a serene beach or
a quiet forest, fostering a sense of tranquility.

Breathwork and relaxation practices share a
common thread: they invite us to pause and
reconnect with ourselves. In a fast-paced world,
these moments of connection are acts of self-care,
reminding us that our well-being is worth prioritizing. They teach us that calm is not something
we must seek externally but something we can
cultivate within, breath by breath.

Ultimately, the breath is a teacher, showing us
the power of presence and the possibility of

peace. By incorporating intentional breathing and relaxation techniques into our lives, we reclaim a sense of agency over our inner state. In doing so, we create not only moments of calm but a foundation of resilience that supports us through life's challenges.

Journaling for Self-Awareness

In the quiet act of journaling, a profound dialogue unfolds—not with the world around us, but with ourselves. Journaling is far more than putting words on a page; it is a mirror reflecting our innermost thoughts, a tool for untangling emotions, and a space where clarity and calm emerge. In a world that often demands outward engagement, journaling invites us inward, fostering self-awareness and emotional balance.

The practice of journaling has ancient roots. From Marcus Aurelius, whose *Meditations* remains a cornerstone of Stoic philosophy, to Leonardo da Vinci, whose notebooks brimmed with ideas, observations, and questions, history offers countless examples of individuals using journaling as a means of reflection and growth. These figures understood what modern psychology confirms: that writing our thoughts can transform them, helping us process experiences, articulate feelings, and uncover patterns in our behavior.

At its core, journaling provides a safe space—a sanctuary where we can express ourselves freely, unencumbered by judgment or expectation. It allows us to explore our fears, hopes, and uncertainties, granting them form and context. In doing so, we often find that the act of writing itself diminishes the weight of our burdens. What seemed overwhelming in thought becomes manageable on the page.

Journaling also serves as a tool for emotional regulation. When emotions feel chaotic or intense, writing offers a way to process them constructively. Research supports this idea: studies have shown that expressive writing, where individuals write about their thoughts and feelings regarding stressful events, can reduce anxiety and improve mental health. The very act of naming an emotion—be it anger, sadness, or fear—can diminish its power, creating space for reflection and understanding.

One of the most profound aspects of journaling is its ability to cultivate self-awareness. By putting thoughts into words, we gain insight into our beliefs, values, and patterns of behavior. Over time, a journal becomes a map of the self, revealing recurring themes and highlighting areas for growth. For example, a person might notice through their writing that they often feel drained after certain interactions or energized by specific activities. These observations, while subtle, can guide us toward choices that align with our well-being.

The benefits of journaling extend beyond the individual; they ripple outward into relationships and daily life. When we understand ourselves more deeply, we are better equipped to communicate our needs and set boundaries. Journaling fosters empathy by helping us explore not only our perspectives but also those of others. In moments of conflict, writing about the situation can clarify our emotions and illuminate potential solutions, creating a pathway to resolution.

The practice of gratitude journaling, in particular, has gained recognition for its transformative effects. By recording things we are grateful for—be they large or small—we shift our focus from what is lacking to what is abundant. This simple yet powerful act rewires the brain to notice positivity and fosters a sense of contentment and resilience. For many, starting or ending the day with a few lines of gratitude becomes a cherished ritual, grounding them in appreciation and peace.

Historical figures have often turned to journaling during times of challenge and change. Anne Frank's diary, written during her years in hiding during World War II, is a testament to the power of journaling as a source of hope and resilience. Her reflections, filled with honesty and insight, offered her a sense of connection and purpose amidst unimaginable adversity. Similarly, Virginia Woolf viewed her journals as a space for experimentation and self-discovery, a place where her creative mind could wander freely.

Journaling's adaptability is one of its greatest strengths. It can take many forms, from free writing, where thoughts flow unedited onto the page, to more structured approaches like prompts or questions. For those new to the practice, prompts such as "What am I feeling right now?" or "What brought me joy today?" can serve as gentle entry points. Over time, as comfort with the process grows, the journal becomes a trusted companion—a place to explore without limitation.

For those seeking to integrate journaling into their daily lives, consistency is key. Even a few minutes each day can yield significant benefits. The timing and format of journaling should align with personal preferences; some find clarity in the quiet of morning, while others prefer to reflect in the stillness of evening. The medium, too, is flexible—whether it's a traditional notebook, a digital app, or even voice-to-text recordings. What matters most is the act of intentional reflection.

Incorporating mindfulness into journaling can deepen its impact. Before beginning, take a few moments to breathe and center yourself, creating a sense of presence. Approach the practice with curiosity and openness, allowing thoughts to flow without judgment. Remember that there is no right or wrong way to journal; the process is as individual as the person writing.

Over time, journaling becomes more than a practice—it becomes a relationship with oneself. The pages of a journal hold not only words but also insights, growth, and transformation. They bear witness to our struggles and triumphs, our questions and discoveries. In this sense, a journal is both a mirror and a canvas, reflecting who we are while also inviting us to imagine who we can become.

Ultimately, journaling is a gift we give ourselves—a moment of pause in a busy world, a space to explore and express without constraint. It reminds us that amidst the noise and haste, our inner voice remains steady and clear, waiting to be heard. By embracing the practice of journaling, we cultivate a deeper connection to ourselves, fostering inner calm and resilience that radiates into every aspect of our lives.

Designing Your Personal Calm Ritual

A calm ritual is more than just a series of actions; it is a sacred practice tailored to your needs, a gentle oasis amidst the demands of life. Rituals ground us in the present, connect us to our inner selves, and serve as intentional pauses that re-calibrate the mind and body. While universal principles of calm can inspire us, the most effective rituals are personal, reflecting the unique rhythms and preferences of the individual. Designing your own ritual is an act of self-care, creativity, and empowerment.

The first step in creating a personal calm ritual is reflection. Begin by asking yourself: What calms me? What activities make me feel grounded, centered, and at peace? For some, calm may arise from stillness—sitting in quiet meditation, listening to soft music, or practicing slow, deliberate breathing. For others, it may be found in motion—walking through nature, journaling, or engaging in a repetitive craft. By identifying what resonates with you, you lay the foundation for a ritual that feels authentic and sustainable.

The ancient Stoics often emphasized simplicity in their practices, a principle that can guide the design of modern rituals. Marcus Aurelius, for example, practiced morning reflection to prepare his mind for the challenges of the day. In his *Meditations*, he wrote, "You have power over your mind—not outside events. Realize this, and you will find strength." This simple but intentional practice was not about adding complexity to his life but about focusing on what truly mattered. Your ritual, too, need not be elaborate; its power lies in its intentionality, not its complexity.

Once you have identified calming activities, consider how they can be structured into a sequence. Rituals often gain power through repetition and rhythm. For instance, a morning calm ritual might begin with lighting a candle to symbolize the start of a new day, followed by a few minutes of deep breathing and a brief journaling session. An evening ritual could involve dimming the lights, practicing gratitude, and sipping a warm herbal tea. The sequence itself becomes soothing, creating a sense of predictability and comfort.

Time is another important consideration when designing a ritual. While extended practices can be deeply restorative, even a few minutes of intentional activity can have a profound impact. A short ritual, such as pausing to take three deep breaths before transitioning from work to home life, can create a moment of clarity amidst a busy schedule. Longer rituals, reserved for weekends or quiet evenings, allow for deeper reflection and renewal. Flexibility in the duration of your ritual ensures that it can adapt to the realities of your day.

Environment plays a crucial role in the effectiveness of a ritual. Creating a dedicated space for your practice can enhance its impact, signaling to your mind and body that this is a time for calm. This space need not be elaborate; it could be a cozy chair by a window, a corner adorned with meaningful objects, or even a quiet spot outdoors. The key is to cultivate an environment that feels inviting and free from distractions. Over time, this space becomes imbued with the energy of your ritual, deepening its significance.

Symbols can also add depth and meaning to your ritual. Lighting a candle, as simple as it may seem, can serve as a powerful symbol of light, warmth, and intention. Placing a hand on your heart during a moment of reflection can create a sense of connection and compassion. Symbols need not be physical; they can also be words, such as a mantra or affirmation, that anchor your practice. These elements infuse your ritual with personal meaning, transforming it from a routine into a sacred act.

Historical examples highlight the transformative potential of rituals. Gandhi, for instance, incorporated daily spinning into his life, an act that symbolized simplicity, self-reliance, and mindfulness. This practice was not only a political statement but also a personal ritual that grounded him amidst the challenges of his mission. Similarly, the Japanese tea ceremony, or *chanoyu*, transforms the preparation and drinking of tea into a meditative art form. Each movement is intentional, each detail attended to, creating a ritual that embodies harmony and mindfulness.

To maintain the effectiveness of your ritual, it is essential to approach it with consistency and reverence. While life's demands may occasionally disrupt your routine, returning to your ritual reaffirms its importance. Over time, the act of engaging in your ritual becomes as natural as brushing your teeth—a habit that supports your well-being and anchors you in calm.

Flexibility is also key to sustaining your practice.

Your needs and circumstances may change, and your ritual can evolve accordingly. For instance, a ritual that centers on outdoor walks may shift to indoor activities during winter months. Similarly, a practice focused on morning meditation may later incorporate journaling or breathwork as your preferences develop. This adaptability ensures that your ritual remains relevant and resonant.

Sharing your ritual with others can add a new dimension to its power. Engaging in a family gratitude ritual, a shared moment of silence with a partner, or a communal tea ceremony with friends fosters connection and mutual support. While personal rituals are deeply individual, shared rituals create bonds that enrich relationships and amplify their calming effects.

Ultimately, designing your personal calm ritual is an act of self-discovery and empowerment. It is a declaration that your well-being is worth prioritizing, a recognition of the importance of creating moments of peace amidst life's demands. By crafting a ritual that reflects your values, preferences, and rhythms, you cultivate not only calm but also a deeper connection to yourself and the world around you.

Your calm ritual, however small or simple, becomes a sanctuary—a space where you can return to yourself, breathe deeply, and find clarity. In a world that often pulls us in many directions, it offers a moment to pause and reconnect, reminding us of the power of intentionality and presence. By embracing the practice of ritual, you create a foundation of peace that sustains you through life's ever-changing landscape.

CHAPTER 8: THE CALM WITHIN – SUSTAINING PEACE IN A CHAOTIC WORLD

Peace as a Lifelong Journey

Inner peace is not a destination that we arrive at and settle into permanently. It is a dynamic, ever-evolving journey that unfolds across the landscapes of our lives. Like a winding path through a forest, the way forward is often obscured by challenges, yet each step reveals new growth and deeper understanding. To cultivate inner peace is to embrace this journey as an ongoing process, one that requires commitment, reflection, and resilience.

The idea of peace as a lifelong endeavor is reflected in many philosophical and spiritual traditions. The ancient Stoics, for instance, viewed the pursuit of tranquility as a daily practice rather than a fixed state. Marcus Aurelius, in his *Meditations*, emphasized the importance of returning to one's principles each day, writing, "You have power over your mind—not outside events. Realize this, and you will find strength." This reminder speaks to the reality that peace requires continual effort and intention, especially in a world fraught with unpredictability.

Buddhist philosophy offers a similar perspective, viewing peace as a practice that deepens over time. The Buddha likened the mind to a garden, requiring regular cultivation to flourish. Just as weeds must be removed and new seeds sown, our inner world requires ongoing care and attention. This process is not about achieving perfection but about nurturing a state of harmony that can withstand life's inevitable storms.

One of the most profound lessons of the peace journey is the acceptance of impermanence. Life is marked by change—relationships evolve, circumstances shift, and challenges arise. Resisting these changes often leads to tension and unrest, while accepting them allows us to flow with life rather than against it. This concept is beautifully illustrated in the metaphor of water, which adapts to the shape of its container and flows around obstacles without losing its essence. By adopting the qualities of water—flexibility, adaptability, and persistence—we can navigate life's uncertainties with greater ease.

Resilience plays a central role in sustaining peace over time. It is the ability to recover from setbacks, to bend without breaking, and to grow stronger through adversity. Resilience is not an inherent trait but a skill that can be developed through practice. By embracing challenges as opportunities for growth, we build the capacity to maintain calm and clarity even in difficult circumstances. This perspective transforms obstacles into stepping stones on the path to greater inner strength.

Historical figures who exemplify resilience remind us of the power of persistence in the pursuit of peace. Nelson Mandela, who endured 27 years of imprisonment, emerged with a sense of forgiveness and resolve that transformed not only his own life but also the course of a nation. Mandela's ability to sustain inner peace amidst profound hardship demonstrates that peace is not the absence of struggle but the ability to remain centered within it. His journey underscores the importance of patience, perspective, and unwavering commitment to one's values.

Another key aspect of the peace journey is self-compassion. The path to inner calm is rarely linear, and there will be moments of doubt, frustration, and difficulty. During these times, it is essential to treat ourselves with kindness rather than criticism. Self-compassion allows us to acknowledge our imperfections without judgment, creating a space for growth and healing. As the psychologist Kristin Neff writes, "Compassion for ourselves in no way releases us from responsibility for our actions. Rather, it releases us from the self-hatred that prevents us from responding to our life with clarity and balance."

The ongoing nature of peace requires us to continually reevaluate and refine our practices. Just as the seasons bring different needs to a garden, different phases of life call for different approaches to inner calm. What brings peace in one season may no longer serve us in another, and this evolution is both natural and necessary. By remaining open to change and willing to adapt, we ensure that our journey remains relevant and meaningful.

One practical way to sustain the peace journey is through the creation of rituals and habits that anchor us in the present moment. These practices, whether they involve mindfulness, journaling, or connecting with nature, act as touchstones that remind us of our commitment to calm. Over time, they become part of the rhythm of our lives, providing stability and continuity amidst change.

Equally important is the cultivation of gratitude. Gratitude shifts our focus from what is lacking to what is present, fostering a sense of contentment and abundance. By regularly reflecting on the people, experiences, and opportunities that bring joy and meaning to our lives, we reinforce our connection to the present and strengthen our resilience against life's challenges.

The lifelong journey of peace also involves sharing our practices and insights with others. By engaging in conversations about calm, supporting loved ones in their own journeys, and contributing to a culture of kindness, we create a ripple effect that extends beyond ourselves. The act of sharing not only reinforces our own commitment to peace but also enriches the lives of those around us, creating a sense of interconnectedness and shared purpose.

Ultimately, the journey of peace is deeply personal yet profoundly universal. It is a path that invites us to grow, adapt, and deepen our understanding of ourselves and the world. By embracing peace as a lifelong pursuit, we cultivate a sense of purpose and resilience that sustains us through life's ups and downs. The path may not always be easy, but it is one of the most meaningful journeys we can undertake—a journey toward becoming our truest, calmest selves.

Building a Supportive Community

Inner peace is often viewed as a solitary pursuit, a quiet journey inward. While moments of solitude are undoubtedly essential, the path to sustaining inner calm is not one we must walk alone. Relationships and community play a vital role in our ability to maintain balance and resilience, providing support, perspective, and connection in the face of life's challenges. By building a supportive community, we not only nurture our own well-being but also contribute to the collective calm of those around us.

Humans are inherently social beings. From the earliest hunter-gatherer societies to the interconnected digital age, we have sought connection and collaboration to thrive. These connections are more than practical—they are deeply emotional and psychological. Positive relationships offer a sense of belonging, reduce stress, and foster resilience. They remind us that we are not isolated in our struggles, that we share in the joys and sorrows of the human experience.

One of the most profound benefits of community is the sense of shared understanding it provides. When we feel seen, heard, and valued, our inner calm is reinforced. Consider the impact of a kind word from a friend during a difficult time or the comfort of knowing that someone truly understands your perspective. These moments of connection create a ripple effect, reducing anxiety and fostering emotional balance.

Historical figures have often emphasized the importance of community in the pursuit of inner peace. The philosopher Aristotle, in his writings on friendship, described it as a vital component of a fulfilling life. He distinguished between friendships of utility, pleasure, and virtue, arguing that the highest form of friendship is rooted in mutual respect and a shared commitment to growth. Such friendships not only enrich our lives but also act as anchors in turbulent times, offering stability and encouragement.

Similarly, the teachings of Buddhist monk Thich Nhat Hanh highlight the interconnection between personal and communal peace. He introduced the concept of "interbeing," the idea that our existence is deeply interconnected with others. In his view, cultivating inner calm is not a solitary act but one that impacts and is impacted by those around us. "When we are peaceful, everyone in our family, our community, will benefit from our peace," he wrote. This perspective reminds us that our relationships are both a source and a reflection of our inner state.

Building a supportive community begins with intentionality—seeking out relationships that uplift, inspire, and align with our values. These connections may take many forms: a close circle of friends, a family unit, a professional network, or a shared-interest group. What matters is the quality of these relationships, not their quantity. A single, deeply supportive connection can be more valuable than a wide but shallow network.

Creating and maintaining meaningful relationships requires effort and vulnerability. It involves active listening, open communication, and a willingness to offer and receive support. These practices create a foundation of trust and understanding, essential for fostering a sense of safety and belonging. For example, taking the time to truly listen to a friend's concerns without judgment strengthens the bond between you and reinforces a sense of mutual care.

In addition to personal relationships, broader communities can serve as a source of inner calm. Participating in a community group, attending religious or spiritual gatherings, or engaging in volunteer work connects us to a larger purpose. These activities remind us that we are part of something greater than ourselves, providing perspective and reducing feelings of isolation. Research supports this idea, showing that individuals who engage in community activities often experience lower levels of stress and greater life satisfaction.

A supportive community also serves as a mirror, reflecting back the strengths and qualities we might overlook in ourselves. When others express appreciation for our contributions or affirm our abilities, it reinforces our sense of worth and capability. This positive reinforcement helps us navigate challenges with greater confidence and resilience.

The power of community is perhaps most evident during times of crisis. In the aftermath of natural disasters, for example, stories often emerge of neighbors helping neighbors, strangers offering assistance, and communities coming together to rebuild. These acts of collective support not only address immediate needs but also create a profound sense of hope and solidarity. They remind us that even in the darkest moments, we are not alone.

For those seeking to build a more supportive community, intentionality is key. Start by reflecting on the relationships and connections that currently exist in your life. Which ones bring you joy and comfort? Which ones feel draining or unbalanced? Consider how you might nurture the positive connections and set boundaries around those that detract from your well-being. Building a supportive community does not mean maintaining every relationship; it means prioritizing those that align with your values and needs.

At the same time, be open to forming new connections. Attend gatherings or events that align with your interests, join groups or organizations that reflect your passions, and be willing to engage in conversations that might lead to meaningful relationships. Building community is an ongoing process, one that requires both patience and courage.

As you cultivate a supportive community, remember that relationships are reciprocal. Just as others contribute to your inner calm, you have the power to do the same for them. Acts of kindness, empathy, and support create a cycle of positivity that strengthens the bonds between individuals. By showing up for others, we deepen our connections and reinforce the foundation of mutual care.

Ultimately, building a supportive community is not only about sustaining inner calm but also about enriching the human experience. It reminds us of the beauty of connection, the power of shared understanding, and the resilience that arises when we come together. In the words of the poet John Donne, "No man is an island." Our lives are intertwined, and in that intercon

nection lies the potential for both individual and
collective peace.

Purpose and Meaning as Anchors

In the chaos of modern life, purpose and meaning act as anchors, grounding us amidst uncertainty and guiding us through turbulence.
These inner compasses offer stability, clarity,
and direction, helping us navigate challenges
with resilience and intention. A life imbued with
purpose is not free from difficulty, but it is rich
with fulfillment, making each step on the journey more meaningful.

Purpose is not a grand, unattainable ideal reserved for a select few; it is a deeply personal
sense of why we do what we do. It emerges
from the intersection of our passions, values,
and contributions to the world. Meaning, on
the other hand, is the significance we attach
to our experiences—our ability to find lessons,
growth, and connection in the events of our
lives. Together, purpose and meaning create a
foundation of inner calm that withstands life's
storms.

Philosophers and thinkers throughout history have explored the role of purpose in achieving inner peace. The Stoic philosopher Epictetus taught that our true power lies in our ability to align our actions with our principles. "First, say to yourself what you would be; and then do what you have to do," he wrote. For the Stoics, living with purpose meant acting in harmony with one's values, regardless of external circumstances. This clarity of purpose provided them with a sense of control and serenity even in the face of adversity.

Modern psychology echoes these ideas, emphasizing the profound impact of purpose on mental and emotional well-being. Research shows that individuals who live with a strong sense of purpose experience lower levels of stress and greater resilience. Purpose acts as a psychological anchor, reducing the emotional toll of setbacks and fostering a sense of agency. When we are connected to our why, the how becomes less daunting.

One of the most compelling examples of purpose as an anchor comes from Viktor Frankl, a Holocaust survivor and author of *Man's Search for Meaning*. Imprisoned in Nazi concentration camps, Frankl observed that those who survived often had a strong sense of purpose—a reason to endure. For some, it was the hope of reuniting with loved ones; for others, it was the desire to complete unfinished work or contribute to a greater cause. Frankl's experiences led him to develop logotherapy, a form of therapy centered on finding meaning even in the face of suffering. He famously wrote, "Those who have a 'why' to live can bear almost any 'how.'"

Purpose also acts as a guiding light during moments of decision-making. When faced with difficult choices, our sense of purpose helps us prioritize what truly matters. It encourages us to act with integrity, aligning our decisions with our values and long-term goals. This alignment not only fosters inner calm but also builds confidence, as we know that our actions reflect who we are at our core.

Finding and cultivating purpose is a deeply personal process. For some, it may arise from their work—a career that aligns with their passions and values. For others, it may be rooted in relationships, creativity, or service to others.

What matters is not the source of purpose but its authenticity. A purpose that resonates deeply with who we are becomes a wellspring of motivation and resilience.

Living with purpose does not mean eliminating hardship; rather, it reframes challenges as opportunities for growth. Purpose gives us the perspective to see setbacks as stepping stones and difficulties as teachers. This mindset transforms adversity into a meaningful part of the journey, reinforcing our ability to stay calm and focused amidst turmoil.

Meaning, closely tied to purpose, invites us to reflect on our experiences and find significance in them. This reflective process often involves asking questions: What can I learn from this? How does this connect to my values? How can this experience contribute to my growth or to the well-being of others? By seeking meaning, we transform even the most challenging moments into sources of insight and connection.

Practices such as journaling, mindfulness, and gratitude can help us uncover meaning in daily life. Journaling allows us to explore our thoughts and emotions, uncovering patterns and themes that point to our values and aspirations. Mindfulness brings us into the present moment, where we can fully engage with our experiences and appreciate their significance. Gratitude shifts our focus to what is abundant, fostering a sense of contentment and perspective.

Purpose and meaning are not static; they evolve as we do. What brings us fulfillment in one season of life may shift in another. This evolution is not a loss but a natural part of growth. By remaining open to change and willing to explore new possibilities, we ensure that our purpose remains vibrant and relevant.

Building a life of purpose often involves contributing to something greater than ourselves. Acts of service, whether through volunteering, mentoring, or simply showing kindness, connect us to a larger community and reinforce our sense of meaning. These contributions remind us that our actions matter, creating a ripple effect that extends beyond our immediate sphere.

Historical figures who lived with purpose

demonstrate the transformative power of aligning one's life with a greater cause. Mother Teresa, driven by her mission to serve the poorest of the poor, found profound meaning in her work despite its challenges. Her unwavering commitment to her purpose not only sustained her inner calm but also inspired countless others to do the same.

Ultimately, purpose and meaning are not about achieving perfection or grand accomplishments; they are about living authentically and intentionally. They remind us that even in the midst of chaos, we can find stability by staying true to our values and aspirations. By cultivating purpose and seeking meaning, we anchor ourselves in a deep sense of peace, creating a foundation that supports us through life's ever-changing tides.

The Legacy of Inner Peace

Inner peace, though deeply personal, has the power to extend far beyond the individual. When we cultivate calm within ourselves, we create a ripple effect that touches the lives of those around us. Our actions, words, and presence influence our families, communities, and even the broader world. The legacy of inner peace lies not only in the transformation it brings to our own lives but also in the way it inspires and uplifts others, leaving an enduring impact.

Throughout history, individuals who have embraced inner peace have left legacies that continue to resonate. Mahatma Gandhi, known for his unwavering commitment to nonviolence, drew strength from a deep well of inner calm. His ability to remain composed under immense pressure inspired millions to believe in the power of peace, even amidst conflict. Gandhi's legacy reminds us that inner calm is not a retreat from the world but a force that shapes it for the better.

Similarly, the Dalai Lama exemplifies how the cultivation of inner peace can influence others. Despite facing exile and the loss of his homeland, he continues to advocate for compassion, understanding, and nonviolence. His teachings have reached people across cultures and faiths, encouraging them to find peace within and share it with the world. Through his example, the Dalai Lama demonstrates that inner peace is not passive; it is an active expression of love and resilience that inspires change.

The ripple effect of inner peace begins with small, everyday interactions. A calm and compassionate response in a tense situation can de-escalate conflict and create a space for understanding. A simple act of kindness—offering a listening ear, extending forgiveness, or expressing gratitude—can brighten someone's day and strengthen bonds. These moments, though seemingly small, accumulate over time, contributing to a more peaceful and harmonious environment.

Sharing the journey of inner peace does not require grand gestures or public platforms. It begins with authenticity—living in alignment with your values and allowing your inner calm to shine through your actions. When others see the serenity and strength you carry, they are often inspired to embark on their own journey of calm. This silent yet profound influence is one of the most powerful ways to create a legacy of peace.

Building this legacy also involves intentional

acts of sharing. Mentorship, for example, is a way to pass on the lessons and practices that have shaped your journey. Whether guiding a younger colleague, supporting a friend in need, or teaching mindfulness techniques to a group, these acts of sharing amplify the impact of inner peace. They create connections that foster mutual growth and understanding, weaving a network of calm and resilience.

Community initiatives offer another avenue for creating a ripple effect. Organizing a meditation circle, leading a workshop on stress management, or volunteering for a cause that aligns with your values allows you to share your journey with a broader audience. These efforts not only benefit those who participate but also reinforce your own commitment to inner calm, as teaching and practicing together deepen understanding and resolve.

The legacy of inner peace also involves storytelling. Sharing your experiences—the challenges you've faced, the practices that have helped, and the growth you've achieved—can inspire others to believe in their own capacity for calm. Stories have a unique ability to connect, resonate, and motivate, making them a powerful tool for spreading the message of peace. Whether through conversations, writing, or art, your story becomes a beacon for others navigating their own paths.

In addition to its immediate effects, the legacy of inner peace often transcends generations. The values and practices we embody today influence the lives of those who come after us. A parent who models patience and mindfulness teaches their children not only through words but through example. These lessons, absorbed in childhood, shape perspectives and behaviors that carry forward into adulthood, creating a cycle of calm and compassion.

The ripple effect of peace is not limited to personal connections; it extends to societal and global levels. When individuals embrace inner calm, they contribute to a collective shift toward harmony. Communities built on understanding and respect are more resilient and capable of addressing challenges constructively. On a broader scale, the spread of inner peace fosters a culture that values empathy, cooperation, and shared humanity.

At its heart, the legacy of inner peace is a testament to the interconnectedness of all beings. The calm we cultivate within ourselves is not separate from the world; it is a part of it. Every act of kindness, every moment of patience, and every choice to respond with compassion creates ripples that touch lives in ways we may never fully see. This interconnectedness reinforces the importance of our individual journeys, reminding us that the work we do within has far-reaching effects.

To create a lasting legacy of inner peace, begin with intention. Reflect on how you can share your journey authentically, whether through actions, conversations, or community involvement. Embrace the power of small, consistent efforts, knowing that even the tiniest ripple can grow into a wave of positive change. Celebrate the impact of your calm, not in terms of accolades or recognition, but in the quiet transformations it brings to the lives of others.

Ultimately, the legacy of inner peace is a gift we give to the world. It is a reminder that amidst the noise and haste, there is always the potential for calm and connection. By sharing our journey, we become part of a greater movement toward peace, one that transcends boundaries and generations. In this way, the calm within us becomes a force that shapes the world, leaving it brighter and more harmonious than we found it.

CONCLUSION: EMBRACING A LIFE OF PEACE AND RESILIENCE

As we reach the conclusion of this journey, it's important to reflect on the timeless truths we've explored and the transformative practices that can help us cultivate peace and resilience in our lives. In a world that often feels chaotic and overwhelming, the pursuit of inner calm is not just a luxury; it is a necessity. It is a gift we give to ourselves, and by extension, to those around us. This book has been an invitation to rediscover that calm—hidden not in the absence of challenges but in the way we meet them.

The Power of Awareness

Our journey began by understanding the nature of inner turmoil. Like a storm that rages within, our minds are often caught in patterns of stress, anxiety, and conflict. Recognizing these patterns is the first step toward change. Awareness, as we've seen, is a powerful tool—it allows us to step back, observe, and choose a different path. This foundational practice lays the groundwork for all other transformations. By cultivating mindfulness and self-awareness, we learn to navigate the storms of life with clarity and grace.

The Art of Stillness

Stillness, we discovered, is not about inactivity but about presence. In moments of stillness, we reconnect with ourselves, finding clarity and calm amidst the noise. Whether through meditation, breathwork, or simply pausing to reflect, these practices remind us that peace is always accessible, waiting just beneath the surface. The ancient teachings of Zen, the contemplative practices of prayer, and the modern insights of neuroscience all point to the same truth: stillness is where we rediscover our center.

Resilience in the Face of Adversity

Life will always present challenges, but our response to those challenges is what defines us. Resilience is not about avoiding hardship but about growing through it. By shifting our perspectives, reframing difficulties as opportunities, and cultivating a mindset of growth, we strengthen our ability to remain grounded. Historical figures, from Stoic philosophers to modern visionaries, have shown us the power of resilience in action. Their stories remind us that we, too, can rise above adversity, finding strength in the process.

Letting Go of What Weighs Us Down

One of the most liberating practices on this journey is the art of letting go. Releasing emotional weight—be it anger, regret, or fear—frees us to live more fully. Forgiveness, acceptance, and detachment are not just abstract concepts; they are practical tools for creating space in our lives. By letting go, we make room for joy, connection, and purpose. This process, though challenging, is one of the most profound steps toward lasting peace.

The Healing Power of Nature

Nature has always been a source of wisdom and healing. In its rhythms, we find lessons on patience, renewal, and balance. By reconnecting with the natural world—whether through a walk in the woods, a moment of stillness by the ocean, or the simple act of tending a garden— we restore our sense of wonder and perspective. Nature reminds us that we are part of something greater, and in that connection, we find peace.

Creating Harmony in Everyday Life

True peace is not found in isolation but in the way we live our daily lives. Through intentional practices, such as setting boundaries, aligning our actions with our values, and embracing life's natural rhythms, we create harmony amidst life's demands. Balance is not about perfection but about flow, allowing us to adapt and thrive in changing circumstances.

Timeless Rituals for Inner Calm

Rituals, we've learned, are powerful anchors. Whether it's a morning routine, a moment of gratitude, or a personalized calm ritual, these practices ground us in the present and remind us of our priorities. They are acts of self-care and intention, small yet profound steps toward creating a life of peace.

The Legacy of Peace

The journey of inner calm is deeply personal, but its impact is universal. By cultivating peace within ourselves, we influence the world around us. Our calm becomes a source of inspiration, a ripple that spreads outward. The legacy of inner peace is not measured in grand gestures but in the quiet transformations it creates—in our lives, our relationships, and our communities.

A Call to Action

As you close this book, I invite you to take the lessons and practices we've explored and make them your own. Begin with small steps—perhaps a moment of stillness each morning, a deep breath before responding to stress, or a conscious act of kindness. These practices, though simple, have the power to transform. Over time, they become habits, and those habits shape the foundation of a life rooted in peace and resilience.

Remember that the journey is not linear. There will be days of progress and days of struggle, moments of clarity and moments of doubt. This is the nature of growth. Be patient with yourself, and embrace the process as part of the journey.

Inner peace is not something to be achieved and set aside; it is a practice, a way of being. It is a choice we make each day, in the way we think, act, and connect. It is the calm we carry within, even when the world around us is anything but calm.

The Gift of Peace

By choosing to embark on this journey, you have given yourself one of the greatest gifts. Peace is not a destination; it is a state of being that enriches every moment of life. It allows us to live with clarity, compassion, and courage. It strengthens us in the face of adversity and connects us to the beauty of the present moment.

As you move forward, may you carry this gift with you. May it guide you through challenges, inspire you in moments of doubt, and bring you closer to your truest self. And may the calm you cultivate within become a light that shines for others, creating a legacy of peace that extends far beyond your own life.

In a chaotic world, the calm within is our greatest strength. Embrace it, nurture it, and let it transform you. The journey is yours to continue.

ACKNOWLEDGEMENT

Creating this book has been a journey of reflection, discovery, and connection, and it would not have been possible without the guidance, support, and inspiration of many individuals.

To those who have shared their wisdom, stories, and insights—thank you for reminding me of the power of resilience and the enduring pursuit of peace. Your experiences have enriched this book in ways that words alone cannot express.

To my family and friends, whose encouragement and unwavering belief in my vision have been a constant source of strength—your love and support are the foundation of my calm.

To the countless thinkers, philosophers, and

teachers—both ancient and modern—who have illuminated the path toward understanding the human spirit, your timeless lessons are the bedrock of this work.

Finally, to you, the reader—thank you for embarking on this journey with me. Your commitment to finding peace within inspires hope for a world that values compassion, balance, and connection. May this book serve as a guide and a companion as you continue your own journey.

With heartfelt gratitude,
Felix Grayson

ABOUT THE AUTHOR

Felix Grayson's journey into timeless wisdom began in childhood, captivated by the stories of philosophers, leaders, and visionaries who shaped the way we think and live. Growing up in a home filled with books, he spent countless hours exploring ideas that asked life's biggest questions—a curiosity that would later define his work.

After facing his own modern challenges—balancing ambition, uncertainty, and the search for meaning—Felix discovered that the wisdom of the past offers profound guidance for the present. This realization became the foundation for the *Stoned Philosopher* series: a collection dedicated to translating ancient insights into practical lessons for today's world.

Felix's writing is more than reflection—it's an invitation to dialogue with history's greatest minds. Through each book, he helps readers find clarity, resilience, and purpose in their own lives—one timeless idea at a time.

When not writing, Felix enjoys quiet contemplation, deep conversation, and exploring the endless pursuit of wisdom in everyday moments.